Possibilities

Awakening Your Leadership Potential

www.oklahomaspeakers.com

ISBN: 0-9641240-8-4
First Edition

Published by: Brown Books, Inc.
16200 Dallas Parkway, Ste. 225
Dallas, Texas, 75248 U.S.A.
972-381-0009 www.brownbooks.com

FOREWORD

Welcome to the *Possibilities*...to *Awakening Your Leadership Potentials*.

The **OKLAHOMA SPEAKERS ASSOCIATION** is a unique synergy of experts who consult and speak professionally internationally each year and are seen regularly across all 50 of these United States of America. In pursuit of *awakening the potentials* and especially the leadership potentials of others we bring you this first ever comprehensive work!

With more than a century of past experience, education and wisdom among them, imagine the *possibilities* of greatness as the new century unfolds before you!

It was from the interactions which I enjoyed as the President of the **OKLAHOMA SPEAKERS ASSOCIATION** in 1999-2000 that lead me to pull together the collective experiences, education and wisdom of these powerful professionals and provide to you some of the best that each has to offer, in this unique and powerful anthology.

My hope is that you will find many ideas that awaken (spark) innovative new energies which lead you to explore the many possibilities within yourself and those around you, that you become the pioneer of your future and not a follower to others!

Enjoy these powerful fifteen special articles ... *Awaken Your Leadership Potentials,* by realizing the many *Possibilities* both within yourself, others and around you every day!

Jeffrey L. Magee
President, OSA, 1999-2000
CMC, PDM, CSP (2000)

www.oklahomaspeakers.com

*"The **real** leader has no need to lead –*

*he is content to point the **way**."*

Henry Miller

"The Wisdom of The Heart" (1941)

CONTENTS

"A

Leader is

a dealer

in Hope."

Napoleon I

Maxims (1804-15)

The ABC's of Great Leadership

by Corbin Billings K.I.D. and Dawn Billings, M.O.M.

The ABC's of Great Leadership

by Corbin Billings K.I.D. and Dawn Billings, M.O.M.

Achieve results.

In the game of leadership, the one who gets great results: wins. Since that is what great leadership is all about, my mom will help me use the other twenty-five letters in the alphabet to teach you some important rules of the game.

"What can a kid and his mom know about great leadership?" you may ask. We know that if you will learn and live the ABC's of Great Leadership, you will achieve results. If you achieve results, we all win. It doesn't get better than that!

Build momentum.

Momentum is a big word for the power of motion. It's the stuff you need to have to keep your dreams going. Building momentum is like riding a bike up a hill. It's hard at first, but once you get it to the top, the ride down the hill is awesome. Once something is moving it's easier to control its direction.

Controlling and changing direction is often what great leaders must do. Once you learn the power of momentum, and how to build it, you can do almost anything.

Carefully chart the course.

All leaders know where they are going and get other people to follow them. That's why they are called leaders. But great leaders create maps to uncharted territories called dreams. Like Columbus, great leaders inspire others to follow them on a journey of faith, but are responsible enough to create a well-thought-out plan for success. The secret to leading others to greatness is to carefully chart the course.

Develop daily.

John C. Maxwell teaches us "Successful leaders are learners, and that leadership is developed daily, not in a day." We learn one of the secrets to great leadership in first grade. It's called addition. Every day, do more, be more, give more.

President Theodore Roosevelt died in his sleep. When they took him from his bed they found a book under his pillow. Even his last night alive, he was learning and growing.

Great leaders develop daily.

Empower others.

Mom says the best way to lead is by lifting. This is one of the rules we learn from nature. When we look at a tree, what we usually see first are the branches, beautiful leaves and fruit. But what holds them up is the trunk.

Mom says, "Great leaders are like the trunks of the trees. They support the branches and feed the limbs what they need to produce a lot of fruit." Sounds like good business to me.

When you want to empower others you need to ask yourself, "How big a tree do you want to be?"

Feel their way.

I learned this rule of great leadership from my mom. She says that intuition (which is a big word for all the things you know in your heart) is one of the most important tools a great leader can use. After all the facts are in, and the research is done, Mom says "there is one final place to look for answers - your heart."

Sometimes your heart will tell you to do something that your head tells you is impossible. If your knees start shaking and you're scared to death, you're probably on the right track. Feel the fear, and then, feel your way.

Give all they've got.

Great leaders give all they've got and then give some more. They are willing to sacrifice themselves for a greater good. The best example of this rule of great leadership is the life of Jesus. Because of his sacrifice, people's lives continue to be transformed two thousand years after his death. His love continues to lead people to greatness through the gifts he left long ago.

What gifts will you give today as you lead others on their way?

Have vision.

Great leaders have vision. Leroy Eims, author of Be the Leader You Were Meant to Be writes, "A leader is one who sees more than others see, who sees farther than others see, and who sees before others do." I say "Who you are on the inside, determines what you see on the outside."

The great man Walt Disney saw a wonderful magical world, an experimental prototype city of tomorrow (EPCOT), where others saw only swampland in Florida.

Who are you and what do you see?

Influence others.

Great leaders produce change without using force. How? By influencing the hearts of others. The greatest example of this is Ghandi. He was able to influence the change of leadership throughout an entire country, all without any physical force.

Great leaders influence the hearts and minds of others to make dreams come true. They inspire and influence others to care about something larger than personal interests and self gratification. They touch lives profoundly and deeply and cause people to be better each day. How about you? Who do you influence and how?

Justify the outrageous.

Great leaders help others make sense out of outrageous dreams. They understand that all great dreams appear outrageous at first. But with vision and an unstoppable attitude, great leaders inspire others to believe that the outrageous is possible. A perfect example of this is a hero of ours, Dr. Robert Schuller. The Crystal Cathedral began as an outrageous dream. Outrageous at first yes, now it's a reality. Why? Because Dr. Schuller is a master at justifying outrageous dreams and inspiring others to breathe life into them.

Keep the faith.

Great leaders keep their faith. Why, because their faith keeps them. You can weather any storm as long as your ship is right side up. That's what faith does for you, it keeps you from being turned upside down by the storms of life.

Keep your faith in front of your fear and there is no telling what you can do. Keep your faith in front of everything in your life and your life will fall into place. Mom says, "Your faith should be as close as our breath." Keep your faith and it will keep you.

Love change, and keep a pocket full at all times.

Most people are afraid of change. Change is unpredictable and often in a hurry. It wants to move me forward before I think I'm ready. Mom says, "When change stops occurring, we die." That made me not resent it quite so much.

Great leaders love change. They understand that dreams are like water. If it isn't constantly moving, it stagnates. Life dies in a stagnant pond, just as dreams die in stagnant lives.

Great leaders change lives and keep the change.

Make a difference.

Great leaders make a difference. I said at the beginning of this book that in the game of leadership, the one who gets results: wins. But leaders who make a difference with those results, win a much larger game, the game called life.

My mom and I say in every talk we give, "We are only truly great when we benefit the lives of others." That is what great leadership is all about.

What difference will you make today?

No plan B.

Remember the movie *Apollo 13*? My favorite part is where the people at the Houston control center figure out that the situation is very bad. The astronauts and the ship are in great danger. Everyone is terrified and confused and they don't know what to do next, when the leader of the command center steps forward and says "Everybody listen up. Failure is not an option."

Great leaders have no plan B because failure is not an option.

Optimize opportunity.

No matter what the situation, great leaders see opportunities everywhere. They understand that opportunities are the result of the right attitude. My mom says "All challenges in life are really opportunities in disguise." She says, "Great leaders know how to make lemonade out of the lemons life hands them."

I say "Truly great leaders are the ones who not only make lemonade out of the lemons life hands them, they then sell the lemonade for a profit."

When life hands you a lemon, how will you quench your thirst?

Pay the price today for tomorrow's success.

The ability to win in any game comes from strength. Great athletes spend hundreds of hours working out for each hour they spend playing the game. The game of leadership is just the same. Skills and abilities are like muscles, you must be dedicated to building today so that you are guaranteed the power and strength you need for tomorrow.

Building leadership muscles like respect, vision, knowledge, persistence, expertise, etc., means that you have to pay the price today for tomorrow's success.

Question others.

Imagine that each person gets a treasure chest when they are born. As we grow we fill it with all the gifts and talents we develop as well as jewels of experience.

When we ask questions, other people have a chance to share with us the gifts and talents they have been hiding in their treasure chest.

Great leaders listen. You can learn a lot from other people. If you don't believe me, just ask them.

Read everything.

Great leaders read everything. Not only are they dedicated to reading books and developing daily, but they must commit to becoming readers of everything. Mom says, "A great leader must be able to read people, situations, future trends, and most importantly their own motivations, but these things can only be read with eyes of the heart."

In order for leaders to succeed, they must become excellent readers with both their eyes and their hearts.

See the best in others.

We usually see in others, what we expect to see. I say, "Expect the best."

When you expect the best, an amazing thing happens, people work hard to live up to your expectations. If you want people to be outstanding, see them as outstanding. But first you must see and live the best of yourself.

People can only be as great as their leader. See the best in others and live the best of yourself.

Take action.

Mom says, "No matter how great the dream, or perfect the plan, they are nothing without action, and action is nothing without a dream and a plan."

All great leaders take action, but not just any action, they take the right action, at the right time. This is one more place where addition really works. Right action + Right time = Success.

How is your life adding up?

Unite with great people.

One of mom's favorite quotes is by Luciano de Crescenzo. "We are each of us angels with only one wing. And we can only fly embracing each other."

Mom says, "Great dreams always begin with great people." And that, "No great man or woman does anything alone." That's why there is no "I" in TEAM. Mom says, "TEAM means that Together Everyone Achieves More."

If you want to be a great leader, you have to build a great team.

Value integrity.

Integrity is a big word for Tell the Truth. Mom calls it being your word. She says that "Your word is the most precious gift you will ever give to another person and only you have control of its value."

Trust is built on truth, and great leadership is built on trust. Great leaders know the value of integrity. It is a part of all they do. It's not easy to be your word and do what you say you are going to do, but great leaders don't settle for easy.

Win hearts.

There's an old saying: To lead yourself, use your head; to lead others, use your heart. Mom and I have a signature song that talks about the importance of winning hearts. It's called To Touch a Life. The job of a great leader is –

> To touch a life in a way that can be counted on to change the direction of a heart and create a better world.

Great leaders understand that the way to win the leadership game is by touching lives, winning hearts and making a difference with your presence.

Whose life will you touch today?

X-perience success and failure.

Great leaders succeed and fail and use both experiences to make themselves better. They realize that their failures are every bit as important as their successes.

The great leader General George S. Patton said, "I don't measure a man's success by how high he climbs but how high he bounces when he hits bottom."

When you stumble, how high will you bounce?

Yield greatness.

Yield means produce or give forth. Great leaders produce results and give forth greatness. How? Simply by living their greatness. People notice.

Thomas Edison tells us, "What you are will show in what you do." If you are great, you will yield greatness.

What will you yield today?

Zoom in on what's important.

Great leaders focus, they zoom in on what's important. If you focus on each of the ABC's of great leadership, learn and live them and give them your best, you will be a great leader and a great gift to the world.

The world desperately needs great leaders. So as my mom and I finish this book we want to say thanks for your dedication. Living the life of a great leader isn't easy. It takes commitment, heart and courage.

Thank you for giving the world - yours.

Sowing The Seeds Of Success

by Randy Carter

Sowing The Seeds Of Success

by Randy Carter

How could I be in such a mess? Completely and utterly broke. I was well educated and a hard worker. I was a nice guy and reasonably intelligent. How could I be in such a mess? It couldn't have been my fault, I came from a good family and paid my taxes. I even did community volunteer work. But at the ripe old age of 27 I found myself completely and utterly broke, not only broke but everything I owned including my home, my car, my furniture and even the clothes on my back; now belonged to the court. On top of all that my partner and I were in debt to the tune of a quarter of a million dollars. How could I be in such a mess? It took a while to figure out who to blame for this mess I was in. But when I was able to narrow it down, when I was able to point the finger at the culprit, when I was able to appropriately fix the blame on the right person I was able to finally sow my first seeds of success.

The Mess

Here is how I got into this mess. Both my grandfathers and father were self-employed and successful business operators and had been most of their adult lives. So when I graduated from the University of Oklahoma with a degree in finance, it was quite understandable that I opened my own business, after all it was in my blood. Instead of concentrating on my studies in the business school my senior year I became interested in photography. My mother was an accomplished artist doing watercolor and pottery. I guess it is not really odd how the things we grow up around have a profound influence on our own lives.

A good friend was the editor of the OU yearbook that year and promised me I could use the darkroom if I would shoot a few pictures for him. I shot a lot of pictures for him and ended up becoming passionate about photography. After managing to graduate with decent grades and a passion for photography, I decided to open a photo studio and go back to graduate school in journalism. The studio became quite successful, I was doing lots of portraits for individuals and fashion photography for the top clothing stores in the area. As a natural result of the studio and my love of art we expanded into picture framing and showing local artists' work. An old childhood friend and I formed a partnership to do the framing and art. He loved the woodwork and I loved the art. We were doing a good business when one day while searching for a source of frame molding my partner came across a molding machine for sale. After very little thought and no planning we bought the machine and decided to make some molding and sell it to other frame shops. What a goal!

At the time banks were very lenient in their credit practices and my partner and I were able to finance not only the molding machine but the cash flow to buy a whole line of manufacturing machines, the raw materials and a staff of about ten people to make this molding we were going to sell to other frame shops. What a grand goal: make some molding and sell some.

It wasn't long before the glamour of being a bigwig businessman gave way to the drudge of traveling uncharted murky waters with no map to guide me. My partner's wife and I weren't getting along and I soon began to dread seeing her at the business as she had begun to manage the gallery and frame shop for us. My real love of speaking, entertainment and performing had begun to resurface. I was even doing some stand-up comedy regularly at a local club. My real dream was to be in the speaking and entertainment business and that was beginning to pressure my daily life. My plan was to get this manufacturing business up and running, making money and sell out my half to my partner and go on my merry way. Gee, I wish I had written that down and looked at it every day.

What actually happened was that I began to dread the thought of getting up every morning and having to deal with this uncharted business. Instead of thinking successful, happy thoughts or making specific plans, I unknowingly began to use affirmations. The chief of which was, "God, I gotta get out of this." I said it over and over. It became my mantra. I would have a run-in with my partner's wife and instead of trying to figure out how to fix the problem I would chant my mantra. Sometimes while in the privacy of my own car I would chant it out loud. Not only was I saying it I was hearing it.

Lo and behold one day my prayers were answered. Or were they? The banker called and said we needed to move our loans as his bank would no longer be able to finance our business. He could tell from our statements that we were spending a whole lot more than we were bringing in. But we met our goal of making some molding and selling it. We met that goal the first month we were in business. Maybe we should have set another goal, maybe something a little more specific. Numbers and dollars and dates might have been helpful.

We searched all over town to find another bank to take our financing but nobody wanted our business. We had big debt, minimal cash flow and no real plan nor passion. "I just gotta get out of this," was not a real strong selling point. Even though I never said it to anyone else I think they knew.

After much consternation and nail biting [let me tell you sometime how I beat that one] we realized that we had no choice but to take personal bankruptcy. I think that is where we came in on this story. That is how I ended up in this mess, at the ripe old age of 27 completely and utterly broke. I was devastated, I was embarrassed, I was the scum of the earth. Being of such sound mind I now realized it was my job to figure out who to blame for this mess.

I wanted to blame my partner. I wanted to blame his wife. I wanted to blame my parents, the bank, after all they gave us all that money. They should have known better than to give a couple of young inexperienced fast talkers all that money. I even half jokingly asked my lawyer to sue my Alma Mater, the OU Business School, for malpractice. I wanted to blame everyone but myself. My bankruptcy, my loss, my utter devastation was all a result of the harvest of the crop of the seeds I myself had planted. I wanted to blame everyone but myself. But after careful examination I realized that every time I pointed my finger at someone else that three fingers were pointing right back at me. That is where the blame belonged. No, not the blame but the responsibility. I was responsible. I did it. Now I must clean up the mess and get my life back on track. That's my responsibility.

I have heard it said so many times that I don't know from whom I heard it first, but I believe it to be true: "It is not so bad to go down, it's only bad to stay down." This story has a happy ending. Not so much an ending but a happy ongoing. They say you don't change until you get miserable enough. Well I guess I was miserable enough because I changed from blaming everyone else for my failure to taking the responsibility for it myself.

Lets look at the word responsibility for a moment. Heavy word. "Who is responsible for this mess?" "That's not my responsibility" I like what Steven Covey says about responsibility in *The Seven Habits of Highly Successful People*: "Look at the word responsibility—'response-ability'—the ability to choose your response." Wow! the ability to choose your own response. I could choose to stay down or I could choose to do something about it. Thank goodness I had a vague dream for what I wanted my life to be. That dream fueled my response to this horrible situation I found myself in.

The Fix

The first thing I realized was that I had created the whole mess myself. I learned that what you think about and what you talk about to yourself over and over you have the power to create. Instead of focusing on building up the business and selling out my part, I kept saying over and over to myself, "I gotta get out of this." The subconscious mind's job is to bring to us what it is we want and need. If you ask long enough and strong enough you are going to get it. For me, when the subconscious got the message, "I gotta get out of this" it delivered in a swift and expedient manner with no frills, no details and no fun. It hadn't heard the message that I wanted to build up the business and sell out my part and live happily after. All it heard was, "I gotta get out of this." It heard it in my thoughts and words and saw it in my actions. I got just what I had asked for and it hurt.

Sometimes knowledge comes with a price, and this knowledge was very expensive. I learned that I am the creator of my own world and that if I don't choose to take conscious control of my thoughts, words and actions then I will run the risk of being pummeled against the rocky shore like a ship who has lost her rudder in the midst of a torrential storm at sea. But even if I am not in the middle of a storm, without a good rudder I might end up at a destination where I don't want to be, doing things I don't want to do with people that may cause me harm. The seeds we plant grow into the harvest of the life we live. If we want success at harvest time we must sow the seeds of success at planting time.

The Right Seeds

"Just what are those seeds?" you might ask. Once I decided that I was responsible for my own life, I realized that I only had a vague idea of what kind of life I expected. As I proved to myself the subconscious mind doesn't do very well with vagueness. I had to ask specifically for what I wanted and I had to ask long enough and strong enough in order to overwhelm all those messages that I was constantly being bombarded with. I realized that Zig Ziglar was right when he said, "You gotta have Goals!" Goals are the destination. Goals are magnetic, they make us attractive to the things we want and expect in life. Goals are what set the direction of our rudder. They are the seeds of success and unless we plant them and nurture them we will not be able to harvest them. Many things have been said about goals and I have discovered that in order for something to be a goal it has to have some MEAT to it. In fact it can't be a goal unless it has MEAT.

The M stands for measurable. In order for something to be a goal it has to be measurable. To want a lot of money is not a goal, it may be a dream, but it is not a goal. It must be specific. One million dollars, now that's measurable. We said that we wanted to sell some molding, we forgot to make it measurable so the subconscious was satisfied when we sold some, no matter how little it was. If you don't make it measurable you will never know if you have attained it. You miss all the joy of reaching the goal. In the political campaigns I have been involved with our goal was to receive one more vote than fifty percent. Now that's measurable. Plus it is exciting when you reach it and you know it. It was easy to tell when we reached that goal. Measuring makes it exciting.

The E stands for exceedable. A goal has to be exceedable because that helps us to build willpower and without willpower goals are a struggle. I always feel good about myself when I reach a goal and I feel wonderful when I exceed it. When we got fifty percent plus one of the vote we felt good but when we got over seventy percent we were ecstatic. We also knew that we had what it takes to do it again and again. That builds confidence and it also keeps willpower strong so that when, on some days we have trouble seeing any progress, we can look back and know that we have what it takes to succeed.

Goals must be attainable. The A stands for attainable. They must be out of reach but not out of sight. A goal must stretch us to accomplish it, otherwise what would the value be? But it must never be so far out there that we think it is impossible to reach. When things get tough, and they will, it is easy to quit when we can't see the prize. If the goal is so far out there that we don't see progress it is easy for the subconscious mind to get discouraged and affirm the exact opposite of our goal thereby attaining a truly undesirable result. I remember once working on a goal that every time I reviewed or affirmed it, my mind would finish with "yeah right, sure you are." My brain didn't believe that the goal was attainable and worked to sabotage my progress. The goal must be attainable.

The T in MEAT stands for Time Limit. If a goal doesn't have a time limit then the mind loses interest because there is nothing to finish. It is like standing between two mirrors and looking into infinity, there is no end, it just gets blurry and we lose interest. In school there is graduation to look forward to but there is also an end at each grade level and an end to each semester. At those stopping points we can look at our results. We can stop and take a measurement. If we don't measure up we need to make some changes. If we like the results then it is time to set some new goals or increase the current ones. It is indeed a time for congratulating ourselves and enjoying the accomplishment. In order for it to be a goal it has to have a time limit.

The First Seed

When I first learned of the MEAT system I was excited and wanted to put it into action but I didn't quite know how. I first decided that since my health wasn't quite what I wanted it to be that my first goal would be to be radiantly healthy, full of energy and vitality. After careful examination I realized that that was not a goal at all because it didn't meet the MEAT criteria. First of all it was not specifically measurable and that meant that it was not exceedable either. It had no time limit but I felt that it was attainable as I was able to hold a vision of myself radiantly healthy, full of energy and vitality.

Thank goodness for friends, needing help I called my friend William Cook to get together for lunch. He had been successful using this system and I hoped he could help me. After a lengthy discussion and his probing questions, I realized that my health goal was not a goal at all. It was a dream, a vision I held of myself. I was at first disappointed until I realized that it takes a strong dream to support any goal. Without a vision, without a dream any goal becomes meaningless because there is no reason to attain it. A goal needs to be supported with a strong and clear why and that why comes from our dream, the vision we hold of ourselves.

One of the reasons my health wasn't as good as I wanted it to be was because my diet wasn't quite where it should be. In order to be radiantly healthy, full of energy and vitality I needed to improve my diet. So with William's help I crafted a small simple goal. It was important to me to try out this new system with something small and simple to prove to myself that it really did work. Many times in the past I would get excited about some new knowledge or system and set these grand and glorious goals and end up trying to do too much too soon. I would become overwhelmed, lose interest and claim that "this stuff doesn't really work anyway." My dream was to be successful.

The goal was simple: "For the next thirty days I will eat one piece of fresh fruit every day." It was measurable: one piece of fruit every day, easy. It was exceedable: I could eat two if I wanted. It was attainable: who couldn't eat one piece of fruit a day? It had a time limit: 30 days and I was done. Now that was a goal, it met the criteria. Maybe it was not a big one, after all I wasn't eliminating world hunger or ending all war as we know it. This goal was a way for me to prove to myself that this system worked. If it worked on this goal it would work on others.

The Cultivation and Weeding

I had my dream. I had my goal. Now I needed a plan. A simple goal only requires a simple plan. First I needed fruit in the house. That was easy, well I thought it was easy. I must admit there were a few nights that as I sat down before bed to review my action log and goals list, I realized that I had not eaten even one piece of fruit that day. I could give up and quit or I could get dressed, jump in the car and go to the store. Thank goodness for all-night grocery stores. Every plan takes action.

Thirty days came and went. I ate my fruit every day, some days more than one piece. At the end of that month I looked back at my action log and saw that I accomplished my goal, actually I exceeded my goal. I patted myself on the back, celebrated and decided to go another thirty days. After reaching my goal the second thirty days I realized that indeed this system does work. I expanded the system into other areas of my dream for my life.

The Harvest

It wasn't long after setting this simple goal that it soon became a habit to eat at least one piece of fruit a day. A habit I was able to create using a simple system that is available to anyone who will use it. Our habits are what truly drive us to success or failure in our lives. Albert E. N. Gray said, *"Every single qualification of success is acquired through habit. People form habits and habits form futures. If you don't deliberately form good habits, then you will unconsciously form bad ones."*

I challenge you to examine your life. If things are not the way you want them (I don't know about you but the biggest room I have is the room for improvement) then look to your dream for your life. Why aren't you living it? Our dreams give us purpose, they give us the why of living. Set a goal to bring yourself closer to that dream. The goal is the what. Put together a plan to reach that goal. The plan is the how. Take the necessary action, action is the who and the when. Review daily and keep an action log. At the end of the time limit you will either be closer to or further from living your dream. You will have results. You will have the harvest of the seeds you have planted.

You have the power and privilege as well as the personal responsibility to have a wonderful life. The most powerful tool you have is the power you hold over the ability to use your own mind. I have shared with you life-changing principles and techniques. I challenge you to put them to the test to serve yourself, your family, your friends, your colleagues, your God and your country, because service is the rent we pay for the space we occupy on planet Earth. I challenge you to sow the seeds of success and I wish for you the harvest of a wonderful life.

Thank God It's Monday

by Victor T. Costa

Thank God It's Monday

by Victor T. Costa

Wherever You Are Be There!

She was in a small room on the twenty-ninth floor building of a major international corporation. This small room served as a coffee shop for the employees that worked on that particular floor. I was beginning to realize and even experience my desire to be one of the happy inhabitants of planet earth, and, my joy index was increasing geometrically. When I strode in early one morning about twenty years ago wearing my "executive uniform" and my President-of-a-Tooth-Paste-Company smile, her countenance was the opposite. I cheerfully greeted her with "Good Morning!!" She responded, "I hate this place." Her already smileless face deepened with despair. I told her she should just go home. Life was entirely too short (at least on this earth) to live so dismally. She wasn't on my staff. She then told me that she hated it there also. She now had my compassion. I just did not like it that she was so miserable. I asked her what would it take for her to be able to respond more favorably. She said "win the Illinois Lottery." I explained to her that our company statisticians would tell her that she had a gigantic, a gargantuan probability of being miserable the rest of her life. "Leave me alone," was her heartfelt, emotional response. Do you think that I did? No way! Eventually I was able to trigger her smile! I loved it!

Living or Existing?

I observed in over thirty years of corporate life that the large majority of working Americans spend Monday through Friday looking forward to Saturday and Sunday only to spend Saturday and Sunday dreading Monday.

Think about that! Precious, awesome and miraculous life is being wasted. The research statistics confirm my observations. The bumper sticker sign highlights the problem concisely yet completely: "If you do not believe in the resurrection of the dead be where I work at quitting time!"

You Decide!

Let me be quick to point out that it is your decision. You can decide to live only two/sevenths or go for all of the seven/sevenths of your life. I have decided that I want to experience all of this living I possibly can. The only way to do that is to learn to live it with all of our heart one day at a time and to start anew each day—ad infinitum!

Not Easy!

What I am suggesting here is not easy to do. It is a tough challenge. However, the financial benefits are extremely high yield! And, get ready for this flash of absolutely fantastic news: the intangible benefits are out of sight—incredibly awesome.

Reality is Difficult to Accept!

When you witness the explosion of life that follows the slam dunk, isn't that a great feeling. The score is nip and tuck. Your team falls behind five points. But then it comes back and ties it up. Then your point guard artistically lobs up the pass to your six-seven forward who slam dunks for the go-ahead score. See, we are after happiness and fun and joy and that is what is going on here. And, I think that is good. I think that is the way we were created. However—a thousand howevers—let's please wake up to the obvious truth that these kinds of times are rare. Life is so much more!!! It is challenge, opportunity, problems, frustrations, disappointments and death—yes, death. You started dying the day you were born.

Gloom and doom? Absolutely not. Reality, Absolutely!

Let Dying Assist Us in Living!

Our impending deaths can be the catalyst to arouse our sense of urgency to wring every drop out of the sponge of life. We all know and say frequently how fast time goes by and how short life is. By the way, one way to abruptly stop time from flying is to fast at least one meal.

I like the aphorism: "When I was born I cried and the world rejoiced. I want to live such a life that when I die I will rejoice and the world will cry."

Actor-Teacher Robin Williams taught his students in the movie *Dead Poet's Society* the Latin "Carpe Diem" or "Seize the Day."

A cartoon grasped the essence of daily living by revealing a boy asking his Dad if he had ever had a near death experience. His mother answered that he had never had a near life experience.

Someone else quipped that "Most men die at thirty and just hang around until seventy to be buried."

Dance!

From the book, *You Gotta Keep Dancing*, Tim Hansel writes: "Perhaps the thing that creates the deepest sadness in me is to watch people continually miss the miracle of being alive. I see people constantly who wander through each day almost forcing themselves, it seems, not to experience life. Like flies crawling across the ceiling of the Sistine Chapel, we're unable to see the beauty and grandeur at our feet. But do we all have to experience tragedy before we can see life's majesty? I certainly hope not. Perhaps the most important thing that I have learned in my journey with pain is the intrinsic value of life itself—the sacredness of each unrepeatable moment. To partake of it is sheer gift; none of us did anything to deserve it. The most tangible form of grace itself is the substance of our normal everyday life. Perhaps it has been worth all the pain just to learn this one blessed lesson."

A Miracle!

To summarize, Walt Whitman said, "To me every hour of the day and night is an unspeakably perfect miracle."

The Solution!

What can we do to live like this every day? I have already said that this is a tough challenge to accomplish but that just making the effort can make you a multi-millionaire and/or an individual with multi-million "utils" of happiness or both.

I Suggest the Following Strategies:

Commit to excellence and integrity.

Stalk, prospect for, mine and above all apply the truth.

Discover and be you.

Learn to listen and listen to learn.

Saturate your life-style with the attitude of gratitude.

Excel with enthusiasm.

Advance with accountability; stamp out the "they" syndrome.

Mentor and mentee.

Network.

Frequent fun and friends forever are foundational fundamentals.

Develop and maintain a healthy self-confidence.

Work wins.

Replace a problem mentality with a solutions mentality.

Redirect focus from self to others.

Improve processes: Eliminate, Reduce, Simplify.

Organize. Use. Tune.

Focus and tenacity are the Power Twins.

Serve with verve.

Plan less; do more.

Confront and conquer fear.

Flush worry.

Personalize tasks, operations, services, products.

Synergize.

Discipline develops.

Increase initiative to improve income.

Control and refine anger.

Think it all the way through: apply logic and avoid emotion.

Remain teachable; it is a top trait.

Respect human dignity.

Chill out. Lighten up. Hang loose.

Maximize joy; minimize gloom.

Have lots of fun including laughing at self—play—be maturely childish.

Hug.

Smile.

Love—the real kind—genuine care—

Internalize the above, own it, by intermittent repetition.

Replace all of the above periods with an exclamation point!

The above strategies add down to the most important concept or dynamic available to those of us who desire that high level of success that comes from attempting to maximize life.

Attitude—Attitude—Attitude—

During the ever so serious and gloomy days of World War II, the following words of a song were born. You can still purchase this song on tape today—fifty-five years after the war ended. Margaret Thatcher, first female to be England's Prime Minister, said that her father raised her on the words of this song.

Those immortal life-changing words are:

Accentuate the positive,
Eliminate the negative,
Latch on to the affirmative,
Say no to Mr. in-between
Spread joy to the maximum,
Bring gloom to the minimum,
You Gotta have faith or,
Pandemonium liable to break loose.

I ask you: "Could any part of your world use some of that attitude?" Who will deliver it? If not you, who? If not now, when?

Just think of the following, penned by Charles Swindoll:

"The longer I live, the more I realize the impact of attitude on life. Attitude, to me, is more important than facts. It is more important than the past, than education, than money, than circumstances, than failures, than what other people think or say or do. It is more important than appearance, giftedness or skill. It will make or break a company...a church...a home. The remarkable thing is we have a choice every day regarding the attitude we will embrace for that day. We cannot change our past...we cannot change the fact that people will act in a certain way. We cannot change the inevitable. The only thing we can do is play on the string we have, and that is our attitude...I am convinced that life is 10% what happens to me and 90% how I react to it. And so it is with you...we are in charge of our Attitudes."

The Seven Basic Habits of Highly Effective People

Dr. Stephen Covey agrees with Swindoll and spends a large portion of his book on compelling persuasion that, to maximize life, we be ever sensitive to the truth that we do not generally control what happens to us but we always have the opportunity to control how we react to what happens to us. And, that comes back to attitude.

Mr. Positive Thinking

Norman Vincent Peale who was a motivational speaker, author, minister and pioneer in combining the medical with the mental believed *"The secret of life is not what happens to us but what we do with what happens to us."*

Personal Power!

Reader, though you may not realize it yet, the words you just finished reading can be the basis for the power in your life which you have been searching for.

The key is to believe and to implement your beliefs. You need to believe in you and in the God that created you. You are greater than you would dare to believe and you can accomplish and contribute far more than you would dare to believe.

Evidence!

This is not theory! It is truth. I have been experiencing it for over thirty-five years in my personal, family and professional life. I have moved from negative to positive. From anger to peace. From a dogged fear of failure to a more-dogged determination to succeed no matter what. One of my key accomplishments is the replacement of fear with courage. That metamorphosis is a pivot for achievement, contribution and fun!

It is true that we are what we think. Over thirty-five years ago I changed my attitude and it changed my life radically. This happened by establishing a priority to discover spiritual truth. I confronted the question, "Is there a God?" I did not know what I truly believed. To pursue this priority I came open and honest to God. I said to him that I did not know if he existed or not. Intelligent people said he did and other intelligent people said he did not. I said to him that I wanted to know for me. Then I began to read and to study the Holy Bible which was reported to be The Greatest Book in the World and on top of that to be written by authors under the inspiration of God himself. I started to memorize some of it and to apply it–lots of it at first was dry and boring—but it was worth it to plow through that part to get those dynamic truths that spoke to my heart and that helped me live and not meagerly either but with passion and joy and success. Today, it is neither dry nor boring. It is explosive and electrifying. The reason is that I made a decision to accept Jesus Christ as the Lord of my life on this earth and I am now convinced it will go on and on and on for eternity. It is unbelievable. God is so often misrepresented even by churches and nominal Christians.

How about you? Someone has defined an idiot as someone who continues to do the same activities and expects different results. That describes my behavior to accomplish my goal to lose weight and to keep it lost forever.

Are you ready to depart from that majority that has never had a near life experience and join that Marvelous Minority that tries to make every day the best possible day for themselves and for all those around them? You can do it! I know you can do it! I did it and if I can do it you can also!

You are after deep, genuine joy and peace and you know it. Everybody is!

Focus and Tenacity!

If you will stalk the truth with the focus of an eagle and the tenacity of a pit bull you will find the truth and with it a life of creative work and fun.

Kay Lyon gave us this metaphor:

"Our yesterdays are canceled checks. Our tomorrows are promissory notes. Today is the only cash we have so let's spend it wisely."

"Wherever you are be there!"

If not now, when? If not you, who?—Start right now to attempt to make every day, regardless of circumstances, the very best possible day for you and all others on your path and you will discover the benefits right now—both tangible and intangible.

Thank God It's Monday!!!!

The Awesome Power Of Attitude

by Vern Holder

The Awesome Power Of Attitude

by Vern Holder

In my years of study during my travels around the world, I've come to the conclusion that: All the points we've ever heard and all the education and training we've ever had about how to succeed in life's endeavors are worthless! Yes, worthless. Absolutely worthless. I think you will agree with me when I tell you, they're worthless unless ... we apply them to our daily lives.

And why don't we apply them? It's our ATTITUDE about putting out the effort to do the right things to be successful. You've heard it before, "It's not what you know, it's what you do with what you know." Apparently we just go through the motions of learning how to reach our potential, but we don't really apply the important points we've learned. A poor ATTITUDE leads down the path of failure.

WHAT IS ATTITUDE? Webster's dictionary states attitude is a manner of acting, feeling or thinking that shows one's disposition, opinion, mental set. In the *New International Version* of the Bible, Philippians 2:5 "Your attitude should be the same as that of Christ Jesus." In Elwood N. Chapman's book, *Attitude*, to summarize his chapter on Attitude and Success, he says "Nothing contributes more to career success than a positive attitude." In today's business, sports and personal talk we hear, "He has an attitude!" They leave off the word "problem" because most people know what the phrase means.

I understand the average person only applies twenty percent of what they hear at a conference or seminar. I thought about that and said, "Wait a minute, I heard a lot of good stuff at the last conference I attended." But then I remembered all the goodies and notes I collected in that little canvas bag they gave me. That bag was still setting between the wall and my desk where I put it after I returned from the conference. I never took time to review the information. I'm afraid most of us are guilty. Twenty percent! Sports fans, that's not good enough for a winner. But don't forget I said the "average person." Do you know what average means? It means you're the best of the worst and the worst of the best. I don't want to be just average and I'm sure you don't either.

The difference in a winner and a loser is their ATTITUDE about applying life's rules of success. You see, most of us have heard many tips for success, steps for success, rules of success, etc. But we are not motivated to incorporate these things in our everyday life. Are we saying "I'm satisfied with my station in life. I'm satisfied with being average!" What are you saying?

ATTITUDE AND SPORTS

There are so many great stories about how determination and a great ATTITUDE made champions out of people with unbelievable handicaps that I won't even try to tell any here. The point is they all had the same characteristic. That ATTITUDE that always says "You can do it. Don't give up!" One more mile, one more sit-up, or one more hour of practice that separates the "might have beens" from the winners. One trait that they possess that may help them carry on in business life is the ability to fail and get up and go on. With all the changes that have occurred with buy-outs and mergers of major companies there are many people that face change. I like an ATTITUDE poster I've seen. It is a picture of a road making a hairpin turn in the mountains. The caption is JUST BECAUSE THE ROAD TURNS DOESN'T MEAN IT ENDS. DON'T MISS THE TURN! A good ATTITUDE helps you make the turn.

Many times we want to blame someone or anyone for our failures. Have you ever heard, "I'd be a millionaire, but I married wrong!" Reminds me of the story of four golfers teeing off on a new golf course. The first three had teed off on the first hole and the fourth guy took a powerful swing but missed the ball. The first three men smiled while the big guy took a second swing. This time the club hit the ground behind the ball and jumped over the ball. The three men laughed out loud! Now the frustrated golfer, who was a rotund type man, made a third attempt to hit the ball but the club slipped out of his hand. His three playing partners roared with laughter. The embarrassed golfer picked up his club and got over the ball again and said, "Boy this is a hard golf course!" We simply don't want to admit it is our fault for failing. Why is it so hard to admit we're wrong?

After one of my strong motivational talks about ATTITUDE, in Ft. Collins, Colorado, a man, in his fifties, came down front. He had tears in his eyes. He said, "You know, you're right. When I was at home I blamed my parents, and then I blamed the teachers and the coaches.

Then I blamed my wife and I blamed the foreman, the company, the Governor and the President is screwed up too! But sitting here tonight, I realized it has always been my fault for my failures." He took the first step in reaching his full potential. He admitted his mistakes. Most people are where they are because of their ATTITUDE about themselves and what they are capable of accomplishing.

I give many humorous motivational talks about the ATTITUDE of workers about safety. At one of the talks to a company in Western Oklahoma, a worker was given a special award for having worked 38 years without a lost-time accident. That is an amazing record and I wanted to know his philosophy about work and safety. I asked him how he accomplished such a feat. He said, "Oh it's pretty simple, I just do what they tell me in our safety meetings and it seems to work." Did you catch the key word, "do"? He just does what he has been told will keep him and his buddies safe! Many times we know what to do to be successful but we just won't put forth the effort.

After I had won International Salesman of the Year in a professional sales club, many companies asked me to give talks where I revealed how I sold. Prospecting, phoning for appointments, sales presentations, closing techniques were some of the things I would cover. Sometimes sales people would come up after the meeting and say, "Well you can use all those presentation methods and neat closes, you're a sales champion." I would ask them if they had ever tried one or two of the techniques I suggested. They would reply, "Well no not really. What I do seems to work all right." I would politely ask, "Then why are you here trying to learn how to be a better salesperson? Why don't you try one of the tips this week and see how it works?"

I know how they feel because I felt the same way. Afraid to risk coming out of my "comfort" zone to try something that might fail. My sales club encouraged me to "step out" and try new updated things. After a while it didn't bother me that some methods weren't as effective as I would have liked. Because I found the precious few that did work helped me make quota and become a winner every year! DON'T BE AFRAID TO TRY NEW THINGS!

I worked with technical people in eighteen countries. My observation was that the common thread running through these sharp people was that they were so much better than they thought they were! They seemed to reach a level in life and just coast. They'll never know what they might have been or how far they might have gone.

At one of my safety talks on ATTITUDE, I met a man with an amazing story. In 1996 Gary Davis, who was 34 years old at the time, fell 130 feet out of a drilling rig and lived to tell about it. He was in the top of the rig "rigging down" as we call it, when he fell. The next time you're on the 13th or 14th floor of a building, look out the window and you'll see what Gary saw! He broke his shoulder blade in five places, broke his collarbone, and broke all ribs on the left side with two puncturing the left lung. His spleen and tailbone were torn out when a four-inch valve ripped through his body. His right arm was broken, his left leg was fractured in eleven places and his left ankle was shattered. Other than that he says he was okay! That is story enough but I want to talk about Gary's ATTITUDE.

In 1998 I wanted to introduce Gary at the end of my presentation at the Governor's Conference on Safety & Health for the state of Oklahoma. I had asked him if he wanted to be introduced and say a few words. Talking to Gary is like talking to Billy Graham. He is basically a shy good-looking young man from Burns Flat, Oklahoma. He is 6′ 2″ tall and weighs about 190 pounds. He said he would be glad to make an appearance. But then he said something very revealing. He said, "You know Vern, I'm kinda smart." He didn't say or mean it in a boastful way. It was more like he was surprised. I said, "How do you mean that?" He said while recuperating from all the surgeries that he had gone through, he decided to try college.

To understand his background, his family had been roughnecks in the oilfield for years and he had been a roughneck for fourteen years. He was surprised to have a 4.0 grade point average at the end of his first year! Do you see what I mean when I say most of us are so much better than we think we are. Gary and I just gave a program in March 2000, and he is graduating with a degree in Occupational & Environmental Safety. Can't you just see him giving a safety talk before some workers? He'll give new meaning to the phrase, "Been there, done that!" He still has a 4.0 grade point average! He isn't just smart. He is brilliant! He has been asked to speak so many times about his accident, that he has joined the Oklahoma Speakers Association. He wants to learn how to be an effective professional speaker. What is your ATTITUDE about yourself? Are we afraid to risk failing to try to reach higher goals? Or are we just lazy?

CENTER OF THE WORLD

If I were to ask you, "Where is the center of the known world?" What would you answer? The answer is: Right where you are now. Do you realize you can go any place in the world from where you are right now? You can go to Russia. You can go to South Africa. You can go to Texas. You could even go to the moon if you wanted to become an astronaut. You're not too old. Colonel Glenn was 78!

Your career is much the same. You have a choice where and how far you want to go. Do you want to be a Doctor? Twelve years of schooling! Do you want to become a bull rider or maybe a computer programmer? I had two friends in high school that wanted to become race car drivers and they did. Jimmy Nix and Jimmy Reese loved fast cars. They studied how to build engines to make the cars go faster and faster. They trained how to be good drivers and they were good drivers. One raced in The Big One, the Indy 500. They both were killed doing what they had CHOSEN as their life's work. I'm sure they could have been successful as engineers or architects. But they marched to a different drummer and chose racing.

You have a choice about your career. It is not necessarily only one choice in life; there may be many as you work your way through a successful life. The following are some examples where I set goals and worked to reach various objectives.

COWBOY SHOOT

In 1988 I was living in Denver, Colorado, and I read in the paper there was going to be a Cowboy Shoot. A Cowboy Shoot is where we try to hit black steel silhouettes sitting on pedestals at 50, 100, 150, and 200 meters with a lever action 30/30-caliber rifle. No scopes, just open sights and shooting from the standing position. Had to wear a cowboy hat and boots. Being from Oklahoma, I already had those. I love to shoot rifles. So I set out to find out what I had to do to become good at this sport. I'm competitive and like to be the best if possible. If not the best, then be the best I can be. If you don't test yourself, you'll never know how good you can be.

I found most shooters used the Winchester or Marlin rifle. Some thought the Marlin was slightly more accurate because it had twin grooves in the barrel. So I bought a used Marlin rifle. It had a rough trigger pull so I asked the gunsmith if he could improve the trigger pull. He became interested and did a fine job of obtaining a smooth trigger pull. I would practice shooting at sunrise, before the wind and mirage came up. By shooting off a bench rest, I found that at two hundred meters a 150-grain 30/30 bullet had a drop of ten inches. Drop is how much the bullet drops below the barrel at a given distance. Gravity is working all the time. Trying to hit a silhouette of a ram with a fourteen-inch chest at 200 meters with a bullet that drops ten inches is hard to do! However, I found that by reloading a Nosler 150-grain bullet that has a boatail, I could change the drop from ten to five inches. I measured and weighed every bullet I was loading; trimmed the case to the exact length; weighed every charge of power as I loaded my match ammunition. I did all that to be good.

That year we had a shoot every month and I either won or tied for first place each match. I took second place in the Colorado State Shoot and the New Mexico State Shoot. The same man beat me by one point both times. His name was Joe Apache. Yeah, he was Indian and worked at the Whittington Rifle range in Raton, New Mexico. He was a professional and very good. I'll tell you how good he was. During one match the wind was blowing in our faces which means it was blowing into the back of our silhouettes. It was blowing so hard that even if I hit a ram in the chest at 200 meters, it wouldn't fall off! We could hear and see the bullet hit the steel but the wind held up the target. Joe was so good, he would hit the back foot of the ram and spin the silhouettes off the pedestal! I suspect he practiced much more than I ever did! I couldn't beat him. But I did my best. We became good friends. I like experts.

On one of the trips back to Denver from our shoot at the Whittington range, some of my shooting buddies said, "You know Vern you're okay now but when you first started shooting with us six or eight months ago, you weren't very sociable." I was startled. I said "Who me? I talk too much! What do you mean?" They said, "Well when someone was on the firing line shooting and we were standing back in the spectators area, we would talk to you and you wouldn't even answer." I hadn't realized it but when I was getting ready to go up on the line and shoot for score, I was really focused. I was watching those black chickens, pigs, turkeys and rams fall. I was getting my "Game Face" on. I wanted to be a winner and nothing was going to interfere. So if you want to be a winner I recommend:

YOU FIND OUT WHAT IT TAKES TO BE SUCCESSFUL IN YOUR FIELD, "PAY THE PRICE" WITH TIME AND EFFORT TO BE GOOD, STAY FOCUSED ON YOUR OBJECTIVE!

SALES CLUB

While in a professional sales club in Denver, called Salesman With a Purpose, I learned the value of associating with winners. We met every Thursday morning to discuss ways to become better sales people. In 1973 I won International Salesman of the Year by applying things I learned at those meetings. One great thing I learned was: IF YOU WANT TO BECOME AN EXPERT, TALK TO EXPERTS. There is a magic phrase that works wonders. If you don't know something, ask an expert, "Will you help me?" If you're sincere, they will bend over backwards to help you.

I was selling professional golf equipment for Spalding Sporting Goods. Spalding decided to add a line of fine, stylish golf clothing for us to sell to the Golf Pro Shops. I had never sold any type of clothing and was scared to death. The main clothing man came to my area to work with me and help get me started. I knew he was an expert in clothing. I told him I didn't know anything about selling clothes and would he help me learn. I told him I wanted to become the best. He knew I was sincere and told me secrets and the finer points of making presentations with clothes that I would have never learned on my own. Yes I worked hard. But I worked smart with the knowledge of an expert. Believe it or not, I sold clothes to every golf professional that I made a presentation! Sweet Georgia Brown, I had fun trying all those new techniques that worked! I finished the year at 400 percent of my quota. I won three of the four sales contests Spalding had that year including a trip to Spain for my wife and me.

You see it doesn't take much to become an expert. With the right ATTITUDE you can do it. Remember, IF YOU WANT TO BECOME AN EXPERT, TALK TO EXPERTS!

COLLEGE

Boy, I had fun my first semester at college. I took study hall, pool hall, alcohol and dance hall! As a result, I made 13 hours of "F" and 2 hours of "D." When you do that poorly at the University of Oklahoma, they send you to the evaluation center. The psychologist looked at my grades and said, "Vern, you made "F" in Chemistry, "F" in English, "F" in Math II, "F" in History and two hours of "D" in ROTC, (Military Science). I don't understand Vern. You scored high on your entrance test. What seems to be the problem?" I want you to get the picture. I was 6' 4" tall, weighed 210 pounds, was wearing my high school letter jacket and blue jeans and I said, "Man, I don't know. I think I spent too much time studying on that ROTC stuff and didn't spread out my study time." I thought that was funny, but he didn't even laugh. Somebody else that didn't laugh was my Dad.

You see my Dad was an old Indian fighter. That's mainly because my Momma was an old Indian! I'm just kidding. We are part Indian. My mother was quarter Cherokee. She even attended State Indian schools. My Dad was really an oilfield worker. He worked 43 years for the same company. He was 6'2" tall, weighed 200 pounds and had forearms the size of your leg. Using those big heavy rod wrenches, that weighed ten or fifteen pounds, every day had built up his muscles. He worked hard. He was a <u>man</u>.

Man oh man, I hated to show him those grades! I figured he'd hit me, take away my car or something worse. He was sitting in his rocker when I gave him my report card. He slumped. Just slumped down in his rocker like the breath of life had gone out of him. Have you ever seen your daddy cry? I was seventeen and had never seen a tear out of this big oilfield worker. He finally looked up and with tears running down his face, he said, "Son you know your mother has a tenth-grade education and I only made it through the eighth grade before I had to go to work after my mother died. You're the first one in our whole family tree to get to go to college. And we'd hoped you'd get an education and maybe get one of those degrees." .....I was stunned. I had never felt so totally worthless. It's the first time I realized how much I meant to my Dad. I had let him down. Up to that point I had never had a serious thought in my life. All I thought about was another piece of chrome for my car, the next ball game, the next party or girls. At that point my ATTITUDE turned around 180 degrees! I made up my mind that wild horses couldn't keep me from graduating from college!

That's the way it is sometimes isn't it. You come to a point in life where you grow up or become aware you're responsible for your actions and change your ways. It may happen at church or work. It might happen at school or the emergency room of a hospital. It could happen while you're reading this book. I hope so.

I looked my dad straight in the eye and said, "Dad, if you'll give me another chance, I'll never disappoint you again." .....I graduated with a Bachelor of Arts degree in Geology, a Bachelor of Science degree in Business Administration and a year's graduate work in Physics. YOU CAN GO ANYWHERE IN THE WORLD. WHERE DO YOU WANT TO GO?

Don't misread me. You don't have to be a crack shot with a rifle, a champion salesperson or have a college degree to be successful. But do you see the common thread in the examples?

YOU GOTTA HAVE A DEFINITE GOAL.
FIND OUT WHAT IT TAKES TO BE SUCCESSFUL IN THAT FIELD.
"PAY THE PRICE" WITH TIME, TRAINING AND EDUCATION.
STAY FOCUSED ON YOUR OBJECTIVE TO REACH YOUR GOAL.

You notice I succeeded in reaching my goals in the three examples I gave. I didn't tell you of the things I attempted and failed. I have many. I could never play the guitar so you could recognize the tune. I had a guitar but I never took a lesson. I didn't practice very much. I didn't have time. I had to watch I LOVE LUCY. I tried woodcarving. Bought a book and dabbled about a year. You couldn't tell what it was I had carved! I didn't have enough time to really study woodcarving. I had to watch PRO FOOTBALL. We've all tried things and failed because "We didn't have enough time." Ladies and gentlemen I've got news for you. WE HAVE ALL THE TIME THERE IS! We all have the same amount of time. How we use it determines if we're a winner or a loser. This is one area in my life that I have to work on constantly. I have too many hobbies. It takes real discipline to use your time wisely.

By now I hope you understand we have a choice about the course of our life. We don't have to accept being average. I don't mean if you're a midget, you can play pro basketball. But most of us know we're not putting out 100 percent every day. I'm not advocating we should have our shoulder to the grindstone all the time. However, we have the opportunity to improve.

I made a sales call on a pipeline company in the Four Corners area of Colorado early one morning. The foreman was laying out the jobs for the day and he told Bill he had to go up on Old Baldy Mountain and get some meter charts. Old Bill said, "There's two feet of snow and the wind's blowing up a gale! You're going to kill us out there on top of that mountain!" A young fellow spoke up and said, "Hey Bill, let's chain up that new four-wheel-drive truck and see what she'll do!" He was going to have fun at work! I love that story because every one of us has had the same thing happen to us. We'll have the same problem; the same order or same job and we have a choice about how we're going to respond to the situation. I've found that many times the difference between being in the "groove" and being in a "rut" is simply your ATTITUDE!

THE PERSON THAT HAS THE MOST INFLUENCE ON YOUR ATTITUDE IS YOU!

DO MOTIVATION TALKS AND BOOKS WORK?

I asked myself that question in January 1998. If a person is truly motivated, how much can they improve?

I hadn't played golf in about five years and I wanted to shoot scores in the 70s again. I got new high-tech clubs, bought books and took two or three golf lessons. I started hitting golf balls almost every day. I had a shag bag full of practice balls and no matter where I was, I hit balls for about an hour. It was January when I started and it snowed on me one time while I was hitting balls, but I didn't stop. I hit balls at city parks, football fields, vacant lots and driving ranges. You see my ATTITUDE was I WILL DO THIS! I WILL SHOOT IN THE 70s AGAIN!

On April 6, 1998 in Liberal, Kansas, I shot 79. The next day I shot 78. The lowest score I shot that year was a 76 at Kickingbird golf course in Edmond, Oklahoma. I played golf thirty times and shot in the 70s nine times. Shooting in the 70s is not headline news. Many men and women do it every day. But I'm a senior citizen. As a matter of fact when I was born, the Dead Sea was just sick! I was about thirty pounds overweight. Both of my hips and my left knee have been replaced with artificial joints. I have more stainless steel in me than a Toyota! I park in the handicap spots in the parking lot. So don't tell me you can't do something. You should probably say, "I have chosen to be average." Or "I have chosen to do just what's required." Or you might take the high road and become the very best at whatever it is you're doing!

NEVER UNDERESTIMATE THE AWESOME POWER OF ATTITUDE!

Human Nature – What Is, Was And Always Will Be

by John Irvin

Human Nature – What Is, Was And Always Will Be

by John Irvin

I was looking through the *Wall Street Journal* right at the turn of the century. Of course, at the time, I didn't realize that I would want to hang on to what I had read. So often, I clip and file and store those things. My filing cabinet is full of articles, clippings, surveys and such that I have never, ever used. I see them, clip them out and file them, thinking that, "Oh, this will come in handy," only never to be brought up again. Last year, I made a pact with myself that I would clip much less and begin to wade through those things that I have stored and be a bit more discriminate with what I keep. So, I didn't clip that one.

Well, of course, this particular article, I've found myself thinking back to it quite frequently. Reflecting upon it now and again, turning it over in my mind as one turns over and kneads home-made bread dough. And, I have to say, that this one particular part has stuck with me, just as that bread dough will stick to your fingers and hands.

It said something to the effect that, looking forward to the year 3000, there is absolutely no way that we can even begin to imagine the advances in technology that may take place. *But one thing can be for certain. Human nature will remain the same.*

Human nature will remain the same.

As we think of ourselves in this next fraction of time, and how we might become better, more effective, more fully reaching our potential and our goals, this may be the most important bit of information for us to remember. *Human nature will remain the same.*

One of the things that I have come to realize in my own quest through life and through the business world is that, I can't do it alone. I need other people. I need their knowledge, their assistance, their help, in order to succeed. And, they need mine.

Simon and Garfunkel were wrong. No man is an island.

We need each other, Even more so in these days of ever increasing technology. One of the frustrations of this modern world that I hear of so often from others is this whole voice messaging thing, Having to listen and choose from a seemingly unending list of menus, press 1, press 2, press 1 again and perhaps never finding the choice that seems to best meet one's needs. One may spend 15, 20 minutes or more . . . I once was trying to find the answer to a technological question, choosing through any number of these messaging menus and then placed on hold for over 90 minutes before I finally gave up and hung up. Not once having spoken to an actual human voice. We need the contact. We need the connection.

Was it John Naisbitt, the author of *Megatrends* who coined the phrase, *High Tech, High Touch*? I believe so. And, he was referring to this exact need. The more technology with which we are faced, the more that we are separated from one another, the more we need to incorporate into our lives this human contact, to touch one another.

It is speculated that the whole road rage phenomenon is due to this separation from others. While in one's car, one may feel as though one is distinct from society, almost protected by this little enclosure, this little moving box, isolated. One, so often, becomes oblivious to those and the needs of those around one, and while in one's own world, the egocentricity of it all may take over. And the driver of the auto begins to believe that he is the most important creature on Earth at that time which knows no limits ... he "knows" that he is the omnipotent being in the moment. *Hell hath no fury like the wrath of an omnipotent.*

"Today, humankind faces a crossroads, one path leads to despair and utter hopelessness, the other to total extinction. Let us pray we have the wisdom to choose correctly." *Woody Allen*

Human nature will remain the same.

What can we do to increase our effectiveness during our remaining years on this planet? Oh, sure, we can update our skills, recreate and reinvent ourselves. We can subscribe to and read our industry periodicals to remain current in the latest happenings of our particular industry.

But even more so, we can realize that human nature will remain the same.

We all have the very same needs on this planet. Oh certainly, there are those biological, base needs. We need food, water, shelter, warmth, sex. But beyond that, we all share some very basic emotional and spiritual needs. We all have the need to be loved and to feel accepted. We want to believe that we are offering a contribution. We want to be listened to, to have an opportunity to share our thoughts and our ideas with others. We want to feel good about ourselves. We want to feel connected with others and to be a part of something. *And, we want to have fun!*

As we contemplate our effectiveness in our organizations and in our lives, we must not neglect the human side of life. Research has determined that the primary determining factor to customer satisfaction is employee satisfaction. *To create an organization that meets the needs of its customers, we must meet the needs of our employees and of our coworkers.* It really doesn't matter where we are in our organization, what position we hold, whether or not we have people under us, above us or beside us. We can do our part to lift ourselves and others up, to help change attitudes for the better and to do our part to make a dynamic and positive influence in our world.

Go ahead, make their day!

What do I mean by make their day? With every interaction we make some kind of an impression. Always. What kind of an impression do you want to make? I say, make the very best. Make an impression that says, you like people. Make an impression that says, you're fun to work with, that you're positive, you enjoy life and that every day is an adventure. Make an impression that says all those bumps and hazards in the road of everyday living won't get you down. Make an impression that you are there to help others.

Lift others up.

We have an opportunity with every interaction to lift people up, or not. So often, in fact, we not only choose not to lift others up, but to the contrary, we choose to put them down. Our words and our actions that we choose actually discourage those around us. Oh, maybe it's not out-and-out put-downs, Maybe we don't say, "My, you're worthless," or

"You sure are stupid," or "You don't deserve the time of day!" No, maybe we don't say it right out, although some of us do. No, instead, we use more subliminal messages. We do it through our body language, a roll of the eyes, a shrug of the shoulders, a sneer, or even just an unreturned phone call. That can do it.

So often, its not intentional. We may not even be aware that we are sending the message! How often has a team member tried to talk, give an opinion or verbalize a problem and you kept your head down and continued to write or read or do whatever it was you were doing? I mean, after all, you've got to get this done! Or maybe you had started to listen, but then began to drift back to your own work, or just look at your wristwatch. These behaviors send some very specific messages and they're not, "I value you."

Many years ago, I worked for a local hospital. I thought I had a great job, it was in the wellness side of things. I had the opportunity of working with people who wanted to be proactive about their health, to do those things that would reduce their risk of the lifestyle diseases that plague our society today. My coworkers were fantastic. They were positive, uplifting and motivated people. These folks knew that they could make a difference in society and in the world. Yes, we would make a difference one person at a time.

My manager was, as a whole, a very impressive person. He was young, motivated, enthusiastic, talented, full of energy and a visionary. What I didn't like about him, though, were his behaviors when we would be in meetings together. He would continue to work, to write his reports or whatever it was that he was doing when we would be in conference. He would not hold his phone calls during our meetings. The phone would ring and he would answer. Certainly, from that one side of things, he would always be available to a customer. However, the message that I continuously received was, *"this is more important than you and your time."*

The reality was that he was completely unconscious of these actions. In his mind, he thought that he was being available to me *and* to the customer.

You see, he was living a part of his life unconsciously. We all do. Have you ever been driving to work or to the store or somewhere and, then, suddenly, you're there! And you really don't remember a great deal of the drive? It's really kind of scary, don't you think? You were driving unconsciously. Your body was driving but your mind was someplace else. We tend to work with others and even with ourselves the same way.

"Wake up!"

That's what Anthony deMello says. Wake up! Be aware! Live your life consciously! Know your actions!

In order to lift others up, we have to become aware of all of our actions and all of our words. We need to wake up and live our lives consciously, to know that every word and every deed sends a clear message to others. We cannot not communicate. Now, what is it that you want to communicate?

Put down your pencil, stop your calls, turn off your cell phone, and listen. Listening is the most powerful part of the communication process. Turn your attention to the other person fully, and as you find yourself distracted, just bring your attention back. Ask questions to show that you were listening. Respond back to the person with empathy. Let the other person know that you were listening by stating a message that indicates what that person is feeling about his topic of conversation. Show him that YOU were listening to not only the message but the emotion behind the message.

If we exhibit these behaviors, we send a clear message that we do care. That this person is important, has good ideas and says things that merit our attention. This is one way that we can build people up. It is such a simple thing to do.

"Few people care how much you know until they know how much you care." *Unknown*

When we are living our lives consciously, we can be fully aware of what we are saying and what we are doing and the impact that we have on those around us. It is important to remember that the vast majority of us really do try to do our best. Most people want to do what is right. They want to add value to their organization. Even when they have done something wrong, the majority of the time, *their intentions were good.*

Remember that, when you are addressing someone. They meant to do well. Their intentions were good. What will you say? Well, many from the old school will take that opportunity to put them down. To insult, belittle and denigrate. Yes, that is what many people do. Are you one? What results do you want? Do you really believe that by insulting and denigrating you will get better results?!

"Wake up!"

Even when someone has made a bad decision, it is important to recognize what was right. Look for any value that may have been achieved and be sure to acknowledge that. Compliment, encourage, build up.

This is the way that we encourage trust, this is the way that we achieve loyalty.

A survey was taken among managers on what they thought employees wanted most. Managers felt that what employees wanted most were salary increases and bonuses.

When employees took the same survey, the thing that they wanted most was sincere appreciation for the work that they performed.

"Girls just want to have fun!" *Cindy Lauper*

Years ago when I was in college, I worked for a social service agency. I took a position in the recreation department because the pay was higher than that of the position I held. As I became more and more involved in presenting and encouraging positive leisure activities I began to see changes in those youths who became involved in the recreation program. As these kids started to have fun in a positive way, their study habits improved, they began to do better in school, they got into less trouble, they set higher goals, their self-esteem and self-concepts improved and they became more positive individuals.

I changed my career path, recognizing the truth that a basic human need is to enjoy life, to have fun.

"The very first premise of business is that it need not be boring or dull. It ought to be fun. And if it's not fun, you are wasting your life." *Tom Peters*

This is where humor comes in.

Ralph Waldo Emerson said, *"If you want to rule the world, you must keep it amused."*

Victor Borge said that, *"The shortest distance between two people is laughter."*

"If you lose the power to laugh, you lose the power to think," said Clarence Darrow.

And, an unknown first grader said, *"Laugh and the world laughs with you, cry and you have to blow your nose."*

Many people seem to confuse humor with joke telling. But humor is certainly a lot more than that. It is a way of looking at life, an attitude. Perhaps we can come to a better understanding of what humor is all about if we take a look at where the word humor comes from. Humor, I read, comes from a Latin word, umor. This means "fluid, like water." In ancient physiology, good health was supposedly determined by the four fluids, or humors of the body. These four fluids were choler, or yellow bile, melancholy, or black bile, blood and phlem. When these four fluids were in balance we were said to be in good health and in "good humor." Illness, sickness and disease were thought to occur when these four fluids were out of balance. We were out of balance. I like to think that our sense of humor is an attitude that allows us to greet life with a sort of "fluid" flexibility. It is an ability to roll with the punches, no matter what life brings forth, and still be able to maintain a deep sense of joy in our daily lives.

It is well documented that humor, joy and laughter improve our mental and emotional health. Laughter boosts the immune system and interrupts the stress cycle so that many times we do not even experience the negative chemical reactions to stress.

"The people who utilize humor do not experience the negative effects of stress. It is the dead-serious types who drop dead," said Dr. William Fry.

Have fun at work

Another way that we can lift others up is to create a workplace that has an attitude of fun. I don't mean goofing off. There is a difference. We can have fun and still accomplish our work. Remember that fun and play can be an attitude. Make your work play and play with your work. If you do this, you may be more productive, more creative, you may be ill less often (Did you know that the number one risk factor of heart attack is job dissatisfaction? And, more heart attacks occur between the hours of 8:00 a.m. and 10:00 a.m. Monday morning than at any other time?), you may develop more positive working relationships with your coworkers, you may develop more positive working relationships with your customers. You may get the title of Mr. (or Ms.) Congeniality!

Someone said, "Life is too serious to be taken seriously."

Do your best to lighten it up. Think about it ... does a serious or worried attitude get things done any faster? Or do they change the outcome in any way? No! Change your thinking.

I run my business home based. Recently, I got up one morning, put the coffee on, went downstairs and turned on my computer. I came back upstairs, poured a cup and then descended once more into my office. My computer screen was blank. I thought, "Oh no." I turned it off and turned it on once more, thinking that this would help. I waited. The initial chime occurred, but there were no whirring and chirping noises typical of the little guy starting up.

I thought, "this could be bad." I realized that I hadn't backed up my customer database or my financial records in about a month. One can make a lot of phone calls in a month.

"Okay," I thought, "maybe it's not the system, maybe it's only the monitor."

Immediately, I called a friend who had a similar system and had just upgraded recently.

"Sam," I asked, "do you still have your old monitor? My system went down, and I'm hoping that only the monitor went out. Can I come by and borrow yours?"

So off I went. On the way, my mind tried to get me to go to a place of "ain't it awful." I refused. I focused on where I was at that very moment. I made an effort to notice the world outside myself. The sun was shining. The air was warm. It was a beautiful almost-Spring day and the redbuds were beginning to bloom. I reminded myself that I was in good health, I had just had a wonderful cup of coffee, I had some money in the bank and wonderful friends. I refused to fret.

I picked up the monitor and drove back to my office, hooked it up and ... nothing changed. Oh, dear. I undid the monitor once more, picked up the hard drive and headed to the local computer repair service. I knew that very often there was a week waiting before they could even look at it!

Once again, I focused on where I was at that very moment. I made an effort to notice the world outside myself. The sun was shining. The air was warm. It was a beautiful almost Spring day and the redbuds were beginning to bloom. I reminded myself that I was in good health, I had just had a wonderful cup of coffee, I had some money in the bank and wonderful friends. I refused to fret.

It was a pleasant drive and soon I arrived at the techno-repair place. I took in my hard drive and explained the situation. The techno-nerd said, "Let me check the battery."

Twenty minutes later, I was back in my car with a fully operational hard drive. All that it needed was a ten-dollar battery which cost me $30 with the installation. I was very grateful.

I know that I was very fortunate in this case. It could have been worse. And, at the same time, I could have made this situation much worse by my thoughts on the way to my friends and on the way to the computer repair store. I could have gone on and on about how this was so terrible, I might have to spend a couple of thousand dollars for a new system, I may not be able to recover my data, I'll have to try to retrace hundreds of phone calls, and redo a months worth of financial information. I don't have the time! And the reality is that those thoughts would not have changed the outcome one single bit. But my drive would have been terrifying.

Control your thoughts

Once again, wake up, Be aware of your thoughts and make those thoughts the very best that you can. Expect the best. And, even if the best does not occur, realize that this is the reality. Negative thoughts and fretting and worrying will not change the reality, only your actions will make that difference. And, then, decide what kind of a "time" you want to have while you are working through the situation. Make it a "good time" by choosing your thoughts carefully. Choose thoughts that will lift you up, benefit you and bring you to peace of mind.

One of the workshops that I provide, *Bounce Back With A Winning Attitude,* helps us to do just that, to train ourselves to develop and choose positive thoughts.

Take time for yourself

The final thing that I want to discuss here is that we need to take some time for ourselves. Once again, with today's technology, faxes, cell phones, pagers, business demands and even family demands, it is so very easy to become overextended.

"He who burns candle at both ends soon is all waxed up."

Remember Steven Covey and the Seven Habits? Remember number seven? Sharpen the Saw. Take time for yourself. Do those things that you enjoy on a regular basis. Relax. Take a nap. Read a book for leisure. Get together with friends and family. Get outside, walk in the fresh air, enjoy the breeze. Listen to the birds. Feel the warmth of the sun, watch it set. Make a list of those things that you enjoy and then schedule them into your calendar. Make an appointment with yourself. Follow through. You can't be much use to anyone if you are stressed out, worn out and burned out.

Stop being a victim

Take responsibility for your life. If you are not enjoying life, whose fault is it? It's not my fault. It's not the government's fault. It's not your employer's fault. It's not your kid's fault, your parents' fault or even your spouse's fault. It's your own fault.

Take responsibility for the condition of your life, your work and your environment. Focus on what you can do to change things, to improve your condition and the condition of those around you. Change your thoughts and your behavior to lift yourself and others up.

Do what you can do now to have fun and enjoy life.

I remember years ago, I used to see a popular bumper sticker that said, *Today is the first day of the rest of your life*. So what!? I think what speaks more genuinely to our condition today is to *live each day as though it were your last*. Surely, you've seen the little story, *If I Had It To Do All Over Again*. It talks about the person who lies dying and is reflecting on how they would spend more time enjoying the pleasures of life and stressing out less. I think this is where we want to focus. Yes, to make your life really fun, enjoyable and meaningful...

"Live each day as though it were your last and someday you'll be right."

The Real "SECRETS" Of Leadership Twelve Keys To Empowerment – The Courage Of Mrs. Tugmon

by Michael Johnson, Ph.D.

The Real "SECRETS" Of Leadership
Twelve Keys To Empowerment

by Michael Johnson, Ph.D.

Why did you really go to college? Can you remember that far back? I suppose there may have been many reasons. Perhaps because it was the right thing to do at the time for our generation? Maybe your decision to get that university degree was based on helping you make a living or to attain proper credentials for a particular position?

Whatever your "surface" reason might have been, I have more than a strong feeling there was also an underlying desire. It is my firm conviction that a large number of us went to college to learn how to...to do what? Well, we wanted and expected a number of things from that educational experience. In addition to making money and earning a good salary, I think we wanted to learn how to help other people.

That "help" might have taken many forms. Some of us wanted to teach, some wanted to work in the helping professions such as psychiatry, psychology and counseling and even those who desired to work in engineering and other more business oriented occupations still realized, I believe at some level, that somehow helping others would be a most beneficial skill to possess.

Surely, the teacher knew that if he or she could help students learn, the lives of young people would be enriched. The counselor knew that if patients could be helped, then naturally, caseloads would grow and not only would that therapist feel as if he or she was engaged in worthwhile work, their savings account would grow as well. Even the engineer must have sensed at an early time in his college career, if he could learn how to properly motivate and manage others, the productivity of the company was bound to increase and all would certainly benefit.

Yes, I believe we all had that secret desire to learn how to manage, to motivate and to learn how to empower...in short, to learn how to lead.

Not necessarily to control or manipulate, but as I mentioned earlier, to help others live richer lives. I believe somewhere inside of us, we wanted to learn how to do that. And surely, with all those books and impressive buildings, with libraries and lecture halls everywhere, the learned professors would simply tell us how we did these things and when we finally obtained that coveted sheepskin, then we could all begin to make the world a better place, right?

And now, I have a question for you. Regardless of your discipline or field of study, when you graduated from college...did you know how to do those things? Did your course of study in college really teach you how to deal effectively with other people?

I certainly thought I was going to learn how to do all those wonderful things and more. I went to school for the sole purpose of understanding how we really helped other human beings. Let me tell you why...

Southern Women and Rodeo Days...

I was raised on a small farm in Texas. Now, we aren't talking Bonanza here...just a little 300-acre spread south of town. Actually we lived in town, but I spent most of my time on this little ranch of sorts, being raised by two groups of people, both of whom had a very powerful influence on me.

The first group was comprised of the men on this farm...my dad and uncles. Cowboys who rode, roped, branded, dehorned and vaccinated all day and they wanted me to be rough, tough and macho. The other group? The women on this farm...wonderful Southern women. They all smelled clean and fresh, looked beautiful, cooked even better and took care of everything and everybody. And they wanted me to be kind and tender. They wanted me to be soft.

So during all of my younger days, I was pulled between these two groups. I felt like a big piece of taffy in my Grandma's kitchen... soft/macho, soft/macho...so, as you might expect, I grew up to be a soft, macho kind of guy. A calf-roper who cries easy. Maybe that's what Jung was talking about with his *anima/animus* business.

Even with the opposing desires of these two factions, my life worked fairly well through elementary school. I hunted and fished with my Grandma and we had great fun every Saturday afternoon, cheering for the greatest living American of all time, who of course, was Gorgeous George, World Champion Wrestler. When five o'clock came, you could bet my Granny and I would have her 13-inch black and white tuned to absolute perfect reception with the help of those high-tech rabbit ears...which everyone knew could cause instant death if you touched them at the same time. And with an 8 x 10 actual photograph of our Lord and Savior hanging on the wall watching over us all, the world stopped as we implored our beloved hero to just whip the fool out of Mr. Evil Incarnate himself, The Masked Marauder. All this action brought to you courtesy of *Texas 'Rasslin*, on Channel Six, Station of the Stars.

Everything progressed along just like it did in Mayberry until I turned thirteen and everybody went South on me. Parents and teachers all changed overnight. My mom, who had formerly been a nice person, suddenly expected me to make up my bed, clean up my room, feed the horses and help out around the house. Frankly, I was shocked. I tried to explain to her that I simply did not do these things. Then, my dad would come home from work and always seemed to help me find a way to accomplish *all* her instructions with just a single look.

And teachers...these people were worse. One day, we're coloring, eating chocolate cake and taking naps. The next day, we're in the seventh grade doing written problems and diagramming sentences... and my downhill slide began.

I made C's, D's and F's in middle school and more of the same in high school. Then, I followed up that stellar performance with 13 F's in college. By the time I was 18, I was a full-fledged rodeo cowboy who had no need of parents or teachers or anyone else in the "straight" world largely because I knew none of this misfortune was my fault. I had been diagnosed with a below average I.Q. and experienced the terrible bad luck of always being assigned only the "bad" teachers.

So, I found myself swimming in the deep dark water in which so many young people become lost. Like so many in every generation, a lost soul with no skills, no desire to obtain any, no prior success to build on and the future did indeed look bleak. But it wasn't my fault. Some people have it and some don't, right? We all know a leopard can't change his spots. I swam in that dark water for three years never finding any shore, much less a safe harbor. Then a miracle happened...

The Rainmaker...

I heard a man speak. A thin, black man in a suit and tie, up on a stage in front of an audience of several hundred. I had never seen him before and I haven't seen him since. I never knew his name...but now I know who he was. He was my Rainmaker. My purpose in sharing this story is to remind us all of the power of the spoken word. We never know who is listening and how much they may need the words we say. I was in the audience listening on this day to a man who spoke from his heart...and thirty years later, his words are still in mine.

After an experience with a very special roping horse named Susie, I made the decision to return to college one last time. An administrative dean decided to give me one more chance and placed a condition on my reentry to the university. "I want you to attend an assembly," he said. "A visiting lecturer will be here tomorrow and I want you to hear him." I reluctantly agreed and wandered into this speaker's session the following day. I stood in the rear of the auditorium and watched as he addressed the group. In a normal voice, without much fanfare or emotion, he simply spun the web of his life. When he finished twenty minutes later, mine had been changed forever.

He told of his early days in Chicago and wanting to become involved in the "gang" culture. He spoke of being a poor student and making nothing but F's. (My ears perked up at that remark.) I thought, "Wait a minute. What's he doing up on that stage if he's like me?"

Then, he told us about a teacher...an English teacher who assigned a freestyle theme. She told his class they could write on any subject they chose and he decided to write on his "career" goals. He wrote in graphic detail about the darkness of the ghetto he lived in. The junkies, the cars, drugs and small-caliber handguns were the central characters of his *bete noire* world. He said his paper became a vulgar and profane document and he wrote it to shock this old woman and offend her sensibilities. He handed it in with a spiteful glee. He was fifteen years old.

Several days later, the teacher had the papers graded and she called him to the front of the room. The other students began to snicker and laugh and he knew he was in trouble. He covered his shame and humiliation with a juvenile bravado and swaggered to the front. As he turned to face the class, they began to laugh louder and he could no longer bear the shame.

"Why are you doing this to me?" he asked the woman, his heart breaking. The class was laughing louder when she held up her hand for silence.

"I don't like you," she said. "Nor do I condone your lifestyle... *but my goodness, you can write."*

And with that she handed him his paper. Across the front was slashed a huge, brilliantly red **A**. "I got you up here to show all of these yahoos somebody who could write. You made the only A in the class. *You have a gift young man...don't you dare waste it."*

And all the students stopped laughing and looked at him with awe and respect.

He went on to describe how that incident changed his life and how he began to feel differently about *himself*. He would receive a Bachelors, a Masters and a Doctorate. And then spend his life helping classroom teachers and elementary school children.

I will never forget his close. He pointed his hand in the general direction of where I was standing in the back of that auditorium and said...

"I may be here for just one person, but hear my words, brothers and sisters...*If I can do it, so can you."*

And standing in the back of that auditorium, my heart took wings and soared away. I believed him...and I never made another B, C, D or F. I too would receive a Bachelors, Masters and Doctorate. I certainly don't share that story to boast, but simply to convince anyone who reads them to truly believe the next two sentences...

If he can do it, and I can do it, guess what? Your child can do it, your spouse can do it, your employees can do it...*and so can you.*

And that, my friends is why I went to college. I wanted to learn how to do what that woman had done for him and what he had done for me. I wanted to learn how to do that for other people.

Unfortunately, I must have skipped class the day they talked about how to do that, because I never learned how in college.

Do I sound like I'm blaming my professors? I really don't mean to at all. They were kind, caring, religious people who did the best they could to teach all of us what they knew about teaching, therapy or managing a business. I am one of them now and realize how difficult it is to teach the really important things in life.

That doesn't change the fact that during my entire college career, no one ever really talked about how to become more successful and/or how we might most effectively deal with other human beings. They required that we know many things about names, dates, facts, figures, theories and statistics but not very much at all about dealing with others. From undergraduate days to the completion of a terminal degree, the only person who ever spoke to me from his heart was the first professor I ever really heard. A thin, black man on a stage, in a suit and tie.

But I do have some good news and the news makes my heart sing. I hope it makes yours sing too. If you could see what I have seen, your heart would soar with hope. *I have found them!* The people who know how, I mean. People who know how to do what that Chicago public schoolteacher did for my Rainmaker and people who know how to do what he did for me. And the really great news is, while they are not common, *they are everywhere!*

After traveling from Disney World to Massachusetts, from Texas to Canada, from Minnesota to New Mexico...after traveling across America with my rope, my guitar and a big, fuzzy horse puppet named Susie 2, (She's my partner. She helps little kids and teachers laugh.) I am beginning to learn how it is we turn the light on in other human beings. I have found some incredibly wonderful people who know how and they are teaching me.

They are hard to spot at first. They look just like other ordinary people. As a matter of fact, they are ordinary people, but they are doing extraordinary things. They are changing lives for the better. Sometimes, you find them in a carpenter's shop, sometimes in a small factory. You can even find them occasionally in a big company, although I must admit that is rare. I have found so many of them teaching school. And you know what? *They are all doing the same thing.*

Certainly, they are unique. (Snowflakes aren't the only thing individualized.) They might have different occupations but in a very real sense, they are all doing the same thing. Once I spot one of them, I sit them down and do an interview. I ask them, "How are you doing what you do? How do you get people to follow you and generate such enthusiasm in others? How are you so productive and how do you reach people?"

And here is what they tell me...here is what I see them doing.

Twelve Keys To Empowerment...
The "Secrets" of Powerful People
Who Touch Hearts, Reach Minds and Change Lives.

1. They are always SPIRITUAL PEOPLE...Now before you think I'm getting religious on you, hold on a second. Some of these folks are Pentecostal, some are Baptists and Methodists, and some don't even go to church. But, they all believe...no, they know...that something bigger than you and me is going on down here. *They see themselves as their brother and sister's keeper.* They see themselves as helpers and they get help from others just like them.

2. They *look for gifts, talents, skills and abilities in others*...This is one of their most amazing characteristics. There is such a subtle difference between these true helpers and others. Ineffective teachers concentrate only on grades, poor supervisors are obsessed with production quotas only, mediocre CEOs focus only on quarterly profit and loss statements. These true helpers, on the other hand, certainly focus on grades if they are teachers, quotas if in a manufacturing environment, and profit if they own a business...but that is not where they begin. Their initial and ongoing *primary* focus is on the *inside* of the people assigned to their care. Their students and employees seem somehow to sense this primary focus and for reasons I don't even claim to understand, everybody's self-esteem inflates.

3. They help others become aware of their gifts and talents...If you are looking for the magic, here it is. Perhaps I should put this one first. This is the key behavior I observe in powerful motivators. Low performers in supervision, therapy and teaching don't have a clue in this area. They are too busy complaining about how employees have lost their work ethic, about how patients really don't want to get better, about how students are just not as good as they once were and generally, how bad the world has become. High-powered people, on the

other hand, are closely scrutinizing their workforce or classroom for *what individuals can do*. When they spot some ability we have, they pounce on that gift and us like a bee on sweet clover. They hold the special quality up for the person to see. It's as if they extract the talent (just like the bee extracts the nectar) from inside us and say to the owner, *"Look at this! Can't you see the ability you have in this area? Don't you dare waste this precious talent. You must share this with the world!"* And our soul opens its sleepy eyes and we are never the same.

4. *They know they have power and can change lives*...These people are not defeated. They know they can empower. They know how. Mind you, they are not arrogant or boastful, but they live by those timeless words found in Matthew 5:16. Let your light so shine before men that they may see your good works...These people let their light shine.

5. *They refuse to let others waste their lives*...This was one of the most surprising characteristics I observed in powerful people who reach minds, touch hearts and change lives. They are not always nice. Once they spot our talent or gift, if they ever catch us wasting it, they let us know they simply will not tolerate such behavior. Now, this is very disconcerting to the protégé. Here we thought they loved us and now they are extremely displeased and they make us very uncomfortable. Sounds Machiavellian, but they *use* that discomfort we feel to move us to action. We know at some level that they care deeply about us and if they are telling us we can do better...for a host of complex reasons, we accept their guidance and take in what sometimes can be rather strident correction.

6. *They love their work*...this is what attracted me to these special people. I particularly wanted to be like them in this area. They do not dread Sunday nights or Monday mornings. They really don't care what day it is...they just cannot wait to get to do their *Work*. Whatever their chosen occupation, it's not their job and not their career, but rather what they *love* to do. What they do every day of their lives is their *Work* and they love it.

7. *They combine strong interpersonal skills with humor to connect*...These folks are happy campers. It's not that they don't experience an occasional bad day, but the slings and arrows of life don't seem to penetrate them so deeply. And I have noticed the most interesting common thread in their behavior. *They all have really strong interpersonal skills.* When they meet you, they have that hand out, those eyes

are directly on you and they want to know your name and all about you. After just being around them for a brief time, we like them and want them in our world. Remember when Jesus told Peter to go into the deeper water? The fish didn't come to Peter...*he had to go find them*. These folks have that idea down pat. They reach out.

8. *They are lifetime learners*...No evolutionary dead ends here. This group is *interested!* In any and every thing. Doesn't bother them at all to learn technology from a fifth-grader. They are readers, they listen to speakers, they love to go to seminars and conferences, in hopes they might pick up some tidbit that helps them in their *Work*. If only I had lived all my days that way.

9. *They are answering a call*...It may not be politically correct but, sorry, that's what I see in every single one of them. Somehow, they have accessed something deep inside and it drives them.

10. *They are positive people*...I distinctly remember one of my first college lectures. A professor began his remarks with, "If you believe in that positive thinking stuff, you are in the wrong place." This group would not agree. Most all of them read self-help books, believe in the power of attitude and choose to see the good things in the world.

11. *They persist in their high expectations*...Again, so many low performers in leadership positions lament about the poor quality of today's worker. They all have a story about how they tried to reach someone and failed, so what's the use? High performers, on the other hand, know a most important thing. *You must try and develop many more people than you actually develop*. Powerful people fail to reach potential protégés all the time...difference is they do what good cowboys do when they miss with their rope. When good cowboys miss, they immediately coil their rope, build another loop and cast it again. They don't catch every steer, but because they try again, pretty soon they have a pen full. High performers keep on trying too and if they miss, so what? They know there are thousands more who want help and would be grateful for the assistance.

12. *They know (and use) the most powerful motivator...ENCOURAGEMENT!* Truth of the matter is, like George Bernard Shaw said, "If you live long enough, *everything* happens to you." Bad things are just going to occur. What do we do when our time comes? We all have a choice. We can sit there and cry and say, "Why me?" (Answer...*because*)

or we can try to get our breath back and get up and try again. Can you imagine how much it means when we are in these valleys for someone to come along and say, "I know you can do it. *I believe in you*." The legendary architect, Frank Lloyd Wright had a memorable line. He said, "The thing always happens that you really believe in. It is the belief in a thing that makes it happen." Powerful people know that is especially true when you are dealing with human beings. Someone believing in us makes us happen.

So there you have it. Nothing mysterious about what they are doing, but so few people do those things. Wherever I go, I can see them now. They are becoming easier to recognize and after arriving home from travels, after meeting one, I always make it a point to write them a letter or call, because I want to learn from them and be around them for the rest of my days. They have so much to teach us and they know to teach the really important things in life.

I met one just the other day. Her name is Mrs. Terri Tugmon and when you read her story, you will see what I mean. She is a teacher and a leader doing extraordinary things. She is spiritual, she looks for gifts and talents and once she sees them, she tells people about them...and the results are extraordinary. See if you don't agree.

The Courage of Mrs. Tugmon

If you look up the word *courage* in the dictionary, you would find... cour-age (kur-ij-) n. 1. the quality of mind or spirit that enables a person to face difficulty, danger, pain, etc. with firmness and without fear; bravery. 2. to have the courage of one's conviction, to act in accordance with one's beliefs, esp. in spite of criticism. (from the Latin COR = *heart*)

If you look up the word *Teacher* in the dictionary, you would find... teach-er (te' cher), n. a person who teaches, instructs or inspires esp. as a profession; instructor. (ME *techer*) (example = Tugmon, Terri)

We all love stories about courage. We love to hear about that lone figure who vanquishes all foes. Childhood tales told again and again almost always revolve around this inspirational theme. Even adults never tire of perhaps this most noble of traits as motion pictures and novels capitalize on our admiration for the wonderful thing called courage.

Like everyone else, I too love to hear stories about courage. About brave kings and fierce knights, fearless soldiers in battle or the lone gunfighter who defends the town even when the cowardly inhabitants fail to stand with him. We just love people like that don't we? To watch them do what they do gives us hope and helps us feel better. We wish we were like them.

Traveling across America performing and speaking the past few years, I have come to realize something. There are a number of people standing right beside us just like those courageous characters in epic tales. They are busily doing their special Work which is all about touching hearts, reaching minds and changing lives every day. They are not brave kings nor do they resemble fearless soldiers. And while they aren't gunfighters, they do sometimes defend against the bad guys even when the town fails to stand with them. Let me tell you about one...

Her name is Terri Tugmon and at first glance, you might not recognize her as a hero...but she is one. Just as brave as Randolph Scott in one of those old westerns or Mel Gibson in one of the newer models. She is a highschool Teacher and she has the thing called courage. She has been in the teaching profession for some time now and has touched many lives. Some have said she is a bit unorthodox in her approach but most effective. She is a loving, supportive person and at the same time, an unquestioning believer in the quality called discipline. No one wants a lick from Mrs. Tugmon.

Several years ago, Mrs. Tugmon was in her first year of teaching. She was eager, ready and prepared to change the world. She just knew all the students would love her and each and every parent would be most supportive. She could hardly wait.

Imagine then, her excitement as she prepared for her first parent/teacher conference. She lovingly baked cookies and made little finger sandwiches for the mothers and fathers who would be coming to have wonderfully constructive conversations about their children. Her husband, a minister, even helped out by preparing punch and agreed to sit with her throughout the evening.

The first parent walked in and Mrs. Tugmon greeted her with a warm smile and offered her hand. The parent did not extend her hand in return, but rather said brusquely, "Are you Mrs. Tugmon?"

"Yes, I am," replied the first-year Teacher, with that same warm smile fixed firmly in place. "And you must be Randy's mother. He is an outstanding young man."

"That is what I came to talk to you about, young lady," said the woman grimly. "First of all, Randy is not an outstanding person. He has many faults. You wrote in red ink on his paper that he was, and I am here to tell you that he is not. You also put a gold star on his paper. I came to tell you never to do that again."

Then the parent leaned over and fixed her steely gaze on Mrs. Tugmon and pointing a finger in her face, said, "I came to tell you if you ever write on my child's paper again that he is wonderful or if you ever put another star on his paper, we will take you to the school board and see that you are fired. Do you understand me?"

Mrs. Tugmon and her same warm smile, replied, "Yes Ma'am, I understand perfectly."

Now, let's pause for a moment here and let me ask you what would you have done in this situation? Pretend you are a first-year Teacher and someone comes in and says something like this to you. What would you do?

Would you become angry and shout? Would you go and tell your friends, "Can you imagine? I was trying to do something nice for her child and she attacked me!"

Would you say something to yourself like, "Well...I certainly won't have anything else to do with her. She might cause such an uproar that I would lose my job and my husband and I both work and we need the money. I feel sorry for Randy but I can't jeopardize my career for one student." What would you do?

We can all learn a wonderful lesson about life, love and leadership from very special people like Terri Tugmon.

The next day, when the school day was over, Mrs. Tugmon called Randy to the front of the room. Head down and eyes averted, the young man came forward, his spirit dragging behind. The Teacher could tell things had not gone well for him at home the night before.

"I have something for your mother to sign," she said softly, offering a piece of paper to him.

The young man took the paper and read these words...

To Randy's Mom,

Yesterday, you told me that I had incorrectly evaluated your son when I gave him one star. After careful consideration, I have determined that you were correct. After observing Randy for some time, I now realize that he is such an awesome child, I have decided to give him thirty stars. Please sign and return to me.

See you at the next school board meeting.

Mrs. Tugmon

Randy turned the paper over and there they were...thirty gold stars shining back at him. He stared at her with unbelieving eyes.

"You don't understand, Mrs. Tugmon," he said in a whisper. "My parents will have you fired."

"And if they do," she replied, "you will always know that someone believed that you were special. You will always know that someone believed in you."

And she smiled...and he smiled back at her.

Randy took the paper home and his mother did in fact, take Mrs. Tugmon to the school board.

And the school board told Mrs. Tugmon to stop putting stars on Randy's paper.

And Mrs. Tugmon refused.

So, they told Randy that he would be moved out of Mrs. Tugmon's classroom.

And Randy refused.

And Mrs. Tugmon kept right on giving him stars and Randy kept right on doing good.

Randy grew up to be a fine young man and is currently experiencing a successful military career.

And Mrs. Tugmon still teaches school.

And we are all better off because she does.

Because there are so many Randys.

The Constructor

by Rhett Laubach

The Constructor

by Rhett Laubach

We begin with one simple question.

Since childhood, has your capacity for compassion towards other human beings widened or narrowed?

I was in Chicago for a convention. I was standing in a long line at the deli when a lady at the cash register dropped her salad on the carpeted floor while paying for her meal. She did not clean it up, the staff did not clean it up, nor did anyone in the line in front of me clean it up. The lady embarrassingly asked for another salad, paid and hurried off, the staff was too busy taking care of their "to do" list to bother, and not a soul in the line moved.

As I got closer to the front of the line, I kept asking myself repeatedly, "why is no one cleaning that up?" Some of the people in the line almost tripped trying to step over it! When I got to the cash register, I cleaned up the salad. My perception is that everyone else in the line did not clean up the salad because they thought it was not his or her responsibility. I believe they acted upon this belief because their capacity for compassion has narrowed.

The issue of how capable we are to help other people in different situations crosses professional and personal development lines. Many people would like to make it into a very diverse and complicated issue. However, I believe it is generally a simple and old concept with far-reaching implications that today's society has diluted. I also believe this issue needs to be addressed more and needs to be publicly identified and celebrated as a core principle that can help us reach personal and professional success.

We can choose to expand our capacity for compassion by taking on the responsibility of a Constructor.

A **Constructor** makes conscious decisions every day to be a part of the solution, not a part of the problem. **Constructors** operate from a service-oriented frame of mind, set of values and core beliefs. The core principle influencing their decision to be a **Constructor** is that it is our responsibility to help our fellow human beings to improve. Being a Constructor holds real value and substantial significance in their own lives and in the lives of the people they help build on a daily basis. Taken to the grandest and most-involved level, the actions of **Constructors** reach beyond you and me and touch our communities, our nation and our world.

Experts believe our ability and desire to help other people has its roots in our childhood. Carolyn Zahn-Waxler of the National Institute of Mental Health notes, "somehow there's a built-in capacity to respond to the needs of others." I believe the conditions and situations of our lives then takes this capacity and either expands or contracts it. For example, if loving, caring people have surrounded you since you were young, your capacity to help other people will probably be higher than someone who has been deprived of those same influences.

I encourage you to really examine which direction your capacity has moved and clearly identify the reasons. I also encourage you to ask yourself the following five questions, Frame your answers in terms of times you have or have not chosen to take on the responsibility of a **Constructor.**

Who are you helping to construct in your life today?

Who have you helped construct in the past?

Who do you hope to help construct in the future?

How do you want to be remembered?

What type of world are you preparing for your children?

I believe the most important profession on this earth is teaching our children. However, the most important responsibility we have on this earth is to prepare a positive, clean, empowering, and safe world for our children and for our neighbor's children. Even though we are all born. with a natural tendency to help other people, to put it into action in real life takes practice and really is an acquired skill. All of us have the opportunity to learn the skills needed to effectively be a **Constructor**. We can take advantage of this opportunity to construct or we can choose to destruct. The important factor we need to consider is there is no middle ground. You are either green and growing or you are ripe and rotting.

The reason why many of us do not take advantage of the opportunity to be a **Constructor** is that position carries with it great responsibility. Many of us are not comfortable with that responsibility or, because of certain life situations, our capacity to help other people has narrowed. It is unfortunate that most people would rather choose to say "it is none of my business, it is not up to me, or ask what will I get out of it." They believe they are walking on middle ground. However, they are actually choosing to live as an instrument of destruction.

Being an instrument of construction in the lives of our family, peers, community, and ourselves is tough. Many times, it is not the most popular or financially rewarding position to take. However, it is always the right thing to do. My hope is the following stories will help to expand your capacity to respond to the needs of those around you by inspiring you to respond to someone's needs today. Practice does not make perfect, but it does move us closer to perfection.

The events surrounding July 4, 1994, ultimately were my main motivation for choosing the profession of motivational speaking. Please note that the issue of suicide is a complicated one. No opinions expressed are meant to **fully or wholly** explain the situation outlined in the story. The following is a true story.

Kris was one of my closest friends from grade school through high school. The last time I saw him was the night of our high school graduation in May 1991. In our hometown of Laverne, Oklahoma, on the evening of July 4 in 1994, Kris was on the phone with an ex-girlfriend living in San Diego, California. The conversation was heated and lengthy. Kris wanted the relationship to start again and she did not. No matter what he said, she would not change her mind. The relationship was not to start again and that is how the conversation ended.

I will not even try to explain what was going through Kris' head after he hung up the phone. However, he took it so hard that a few minutes later, he forced himself to make an unfortunate decision. His decision was whether or not to take his life with a shotgun. Kris made the wrong choice, put the shotgun to his head, and pulled the trigger. On the night of July 4, 1994, my friend Kris committed suicide and he was gone.

Again, the issue of why people turn to suicide is a complicated one. Just as complicated is the issue of how we prevent suicide. What could have happened before July 4, 1994, to prevent this tragedy? I have asked myself this question many times since. I always come back to three words - Faith, Hope, Love.

For brevity purposes, let us focus on Kris' faith or his lack thereof. For Kris to make this decision, he obviously felt like he had no hope. This feeling of no hope is an offspring of the absence of real, active love and of the absence of faith. He had no faith in himself or in the people around him. I believe this lack of faith was caused by no one stepping forward to be a positive influence in his life. The people surrounding Kris and influencing Kris did not have a sufficient capacity to respond to his needs. They either felt he ultimately was not their responsibility, they couldn't make a difference anyway, they just didn't want to get involved, or they didn't feel comfortable getting involved.

Yet, it is dangerous for us to not get involved in the lives of the people around us. We must take advantage of every opportunity to be an instrument of construction. It is our responsibility and, yes, we can make a difference. Not a day goes by that I wish I had taken on the role of being a **Constructor** in Kris' life.

Get involved in the lives of the people around you. Right now, write down at least three people who you know either personally or professionally that you can be either a silent or an active **Constructor** in their lives. Make a personal commitment to do at least one thing every day to help build these people up. Practice does not make perfect, but practice does move us closer to perfection.

The following story is also true and clearly illustrates the pure joy we can all feel when we actively take on the role of a **Constructor** in someone else's life.

Then there were two – his wife and the nurse assigned to care for his every need. The old man had no other friends left. Everyone else that had crossed his path during his life had stopped coming to see him. Imagine if you went through your entire day, every day, knowing that everyone had abandoned you except two people. It is a lonely and sad place to be. Moreover, of those two people, one had no one else except you and the other was paid to see you.

So was the life of this old man stricken with cancer. A cancer so advanced throughout his body he could not move any of his limbs or fingers. He could not even talk because of the paralyzing nature of the cancer. In fact, he had not moved a muscle on his own for many weeks. He was stricken to the hospital bed and could only wait until the day the cancer would take his life.

Therefore, every day his wife would come and visit. Without fail she would be in his room for many hours every day. Only her visits provided no comfort for him. She would come into his room, walk right past his bed and sit in the corner of the room. She would sit in her chair and stare out the window. Every day would be the same routine. She would not look at him, she would not talk to him, and she would barely acknowledge that he was even there. It was almost as if the cancer had entered her body and was stealing the life from her a little more every day.

The only real friend the old man had was the nurse assigned to care for him. Every day she would be there to take care of his every need. Yet, she did not only bathe him, feed him, and take care of all the items on the hospital's "to do list," she took the caring of this old man a step further. This special nurse would talk to him, hold his hand, tell him stories, and share events from her life. She was more than just his nurse. She was his friend.

However, the old man could not talk, he could not move. He had no way of showing this nurse that he cared or appreciated what she was doing for him. He may not have cared at all. He could have been just lying there waiting to die, mad at the world and mad at God for bringing this terrible cancer to take away his life. Yet, she continued not because it was her job, but rather because she was a **Constructor.** Her life was full every day because she was helping this man. Moreover, it really did not matter whether she knew how he felt or not.

One day the nurse found out exactly how he felt. One day she was in his room working on something and out of the corner of her eyes she saw his finger move. It looked like he was motioning her over to the bed and, since she had not seen him move for weeks, she rushed right next to his bed. Another motion of his finger drew her even closer. She moved right up next to him, putting her ear next to his lips expecting him to say something. When she was right next to him, he lifted his weak arms and gave her a delicate, yet powerful hug.

At that moment, the nurse also became paralyzed. She could not believe it. This weak man must have been saving up his energy all these weeks just for the simple reason of showing her that he did indeed care. The raising of his arms caused him great pain, but he did not seem to care. She meant the world to him and he wanted to make sure she knew. They stayed in their embrace for a number of moments. Maybe because he was too weak to remove his arms again, but mostly because they were both entranced by the moment. As they were embracing, they began to share tears. After a few minutes, the nurse could not tell which tears were hers and which were his.

In that moment, she was immeasurably rewarded for all her hard work and for her choice to live as an instrument of construction in the life of the old man and many, many others. With his hug, the old man was saying thank you. Thank you for caring. Thank you for living your life such that those within your circle of influence lead more fulfilled and better lives because of you. Thank you for making a difference. Thank you for being a part of the solution, not of the problem. Thank you for being my friend.

This story holds a special place in my life because that nurse is my mother, Annette Laubach. The greatest role model a young man can have, she has forgotten more about compassion and empathy than most people ever learn. She is a shining example of the enormous value choosing to take on the role of a **Constructor** can add to our lives and to the lives of those around us.

Taking on the responsibility of helping others is not easy and sometimes can be uncomfortable. However, when we make the decision to do the uncomfortable things and make the uncomfortable choices, we are on our way to making a difference. I hope you are making a positive difference in someone's life today. I hope you are making someone else's time on this earth more meaningful and more joyful because you have accepted the responsibility of being a **Constructor** in their life.

The power lies in believing that you can change lives and that you can build a better you in the process. Once these changes start to occur, you will be rewarded with an overwhelming feeling of personal satisfaction. You will also be accepting an enormously important position in this world – the **Constructor**.

Every day we are given the gift of a new day filled with opportunity. Take your gift and use it to build. Choose to be a **Constructor!**

Who Got On Your Mental Teeter-Totter Of Life? Your Leadership Advantage!

by Jeff Magee

(excerpt from recent book –
Coaching For Impact©)

Who Got On Your Mental Teeter-Totter Of Life? Your Leadership Advantage!

by Jeff Magee

All of the rules of leadership engagement can immediately be overridden by the igniting of one's *emotions*. For the leader/manager/coach, understanding what influences emotions and how they in-turn shape and influence one's behavioral responses, can make the difference between effective interactions and the need for a mediator to deal with the presence of impending or present conflicts, confrontation, stress and even the difficult player taking over and undermining organizational goals.

Emotions, and the wide variance of those emotions which individuals within an organization may experience, including the leader, may be likened to a roller coaster at times – with definite peaks, valleys, falls and level areas. The ability to manage those emotions especially when the mix of generational segmentations come together to comprise a group, is paramount for effective leadership/management/organizational coaching!

To have a common understanding of emotions, where they rise from within an individual, how they are shaped, and what manifests them, may require some elementary understanding by the leader within you, of what each member to a team/group/organization brings with them – in terms of mental baggage.

Emotional Intelligence© showed the world that an individual is more than the sum of his/her intellectual intelligence, that in fact it may be more so of their emotional intelligence which propels oneself.

The effective leader must understand this dynamic – emotions, especially if the goal is to determine ways to engage the individual to stimulate peak performance from them, and to move beyond individual coaching and bring individuals together into one cohesive group for maximum integration and productive lasting results.

To do this, consider the architecture of the human brain.

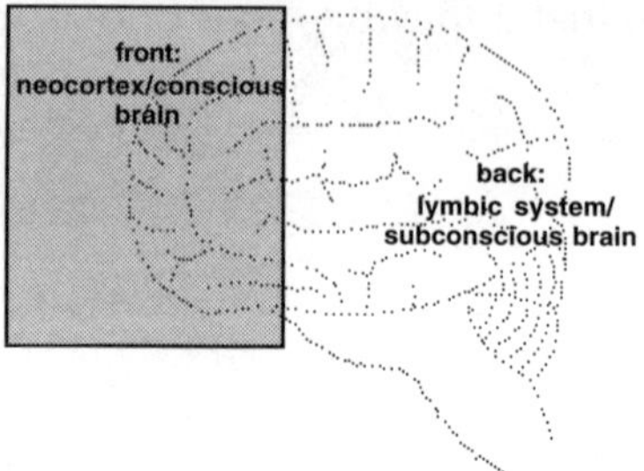

Simply put, there are two sides or portions to the human brain. A front portion, known as the neocortex (conscious brain), responsible for new learning. A back portion, known as the limbic system (subconscious brain), responsible for memories, habits, emotions. If you observe the brain architecture from afar, you notice that the front portion constitutes about 6-to-17 percent of the total brain mass. The back portion constitutes the balance – a much larger and more powerful machine.

With the subconscious brain mass comprising the larger matter, it is easy to see why:

- Habits are difficult to change.
- Emotions can override logic.

In coaching the emotional variance of both an individual and team, it is necessary to understand what one is up against as a leader.

Therefore, to understand one's emotions, it helps to understand the generational segmentations, as each is shaped by the elements that comprised their generation and overall these forces shape and influence how each individual may see themselves and those around them. This also aids in beginning to explain how one interprets things around them and how they will therefore act or react.

The leader must coach the emotional variances to take that "roller coaster ride" and level it out as often as possible, and make the climbs and falls as minimal as possible among others.

Understanding the emotional variances, in respect to what forces may be at work shaping them from the past, the present and how to coach it in the future, takes the leader to the level of viewing the limbic system (subconscious brain) as a sort of teeter-totter (i.e., seesaw) model.

Effective *leadership* of the emotional variances of individuals, and understanding that it may be more of one's emotions which influence instinct, mental/gut hunches, perceptions and views, is inherent to today's successful leadership. This influences how you talk with others and how you engage and manage that dynamic and establishes the working framework for relationships among individuals and how one may engage and coach an individual through developmental stages within an organization and life as a whole.

To understand these emotional variances, one need look to the subconscious portion of the brain and then explore the historical variables within an individual, to determine what factors may be influencing them and what factors over a period of time into the future would either reinforce your earlier perceptions or what factors over a period of time into the future may stimulate and influence a different set of emotions to resonate from that individual.

View the variables within yourself as the leader and the variables within the individuals which you need to or wish to coach via a teeter-totter visualization (or based upon your regionalization this may be called a children's playground "seesaw").

The following diagram places the variables stored within your subconscious brain into two categories on the mental teeter-totter, and based upon what items you have stacked up upon your mental teeter-totter, those variables trigger different types of and levels of emotions to radiate outward from your being – these emotions thus trigger very specific behaviors/actions/reactions from your body.

Remember, every experience you have ever had, word you have read, flavor you have tasted, sound you have heard, view you have seen, dream you have remembered, thing you have felt, etc., is stored in your subconscious brain and is thus stacked up upon the mental teeter-totter. What do you know of your variables and those that you coach?

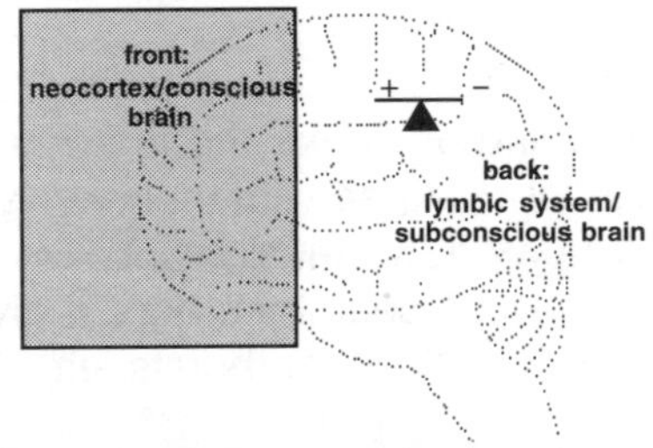

As you review the above teeter-totter model, it would imply that the variables, forces, stimulants stacked up upon that balance beam are relatively even, thus the beam is balanced and one would expect that this individual would be a relatively emotion-even person.

The variances with this individual's emotions would be relatively stable and problems would not be typical. However, most individuals that you will be coaching have a balance beam of life "stuff" stacked upon it that tends to cause the beam to lean in one direction more so than the other!

To validate this model and concept, think of an individual in your professional or personal life that you interact with, which you like and tend to get along with fairly well, more often than not. With that person in mind, do you see that you know some, a lot or maybe you even believe all of what is stacked up on their mental teeter-totter – i.e., you know some history about them, where they're from in terms of where they have lived and were raised, past jobs and positions/titles, level of education/schools attended or not, friends and family members or not, relationships, hobbies and things that they do when they're not around you?

Most of the people that you coach that you would categorize as "likable," tend to be the very people that you do know something about, and because of this you can anticipate what triggers differing emotions to radiate outward from them (some people would refer to these as an individual's "buttons" or "triggers").

So, armed with this knowledge you know what to do and what to avoid in their presence. Do you agree?

On the other side of the spectrum, with the individuals in our lives and those that we coach, which we tend to have difficulty, a lot of the time it may be due to the opposite of what we just discussed – you don't know much about what is on their mental teeter-totter of life!

Knowing what variables may be on that teeter-totter doesn't imply that you have to like or dislike the individual, nor does it imply that you have to agree or disagree with their views. It merely gives you as the coach a valuable window-of-insight into what may be causing or cause certain emotions to be seen by others. It gives you insight as to what may cause certain emotional outbursts, etc., thereby allowing the leader to coach positive productive actions to the emotional triggers which one possesses.

And, the leader also serves to coach an individual to being capable of managing the triggers in an environment and around others on the team or within an organization, to being capable of showcasing (demonstrating) their best behaviors when emotions could otherwise influence counterproductive actions!

Coaching improved behavior rests with the leader's ability to understand the emotional variances of each generational segmentation and how those emotions in turn directly influence the behaviors of action and reaction which radiate from each individual one encounters. As individuals evolve through daily activities and engage others, emotions influence how things, situations and people are viewed. This *"Continuum of Awareness"* illustrates how internal emotions (especially negative emotions harbored) stimulates very exacting behaviors – actions!

Visualizing how best to coach these emotional variances can best be seen in understanding the quantity, quality and diversity of items stacked up upon one's mental teeter-totter – in psychology this is referred to as *apperceptive-mass*. This apperceptive-mass influences and guides individuals to performance or is a primary contributing factor to what holds one back.

The leader must first work within the perimeters of what one brings to the relationship, and then, second, work to influence growth and productive apperceptive-mass to be built upon that mental teeter-totter.

This is done by coaching an individual to accomplishment, demonstrating that individuals can succeed, delegating tasks to individuals which the coach knows the individual can embrace, learn from, be challenged by and ultimately succeed with. THIS, the leader feels, feeds the hunger of emotions within oneself and stimulates greater positive behaviors – actions!

Coaching the emotional variances within an individual (and within yourself) can be attained by seeking those opportunities, engaging in environments and surrounding oneself with individuals which influence (or reinforce) positive emotions and adds to the positive *apperceptive-mass* of the mental teeter-totter. The effective leader continually strives to amass greater apperceptive-mass in a positive direction for each member of the team, as opposed to allowing individuals to have counter weighing negative *apperceptive-mass* – knowing that this mass is what triggers both emotions and subsequently actions or reactions from individuals.

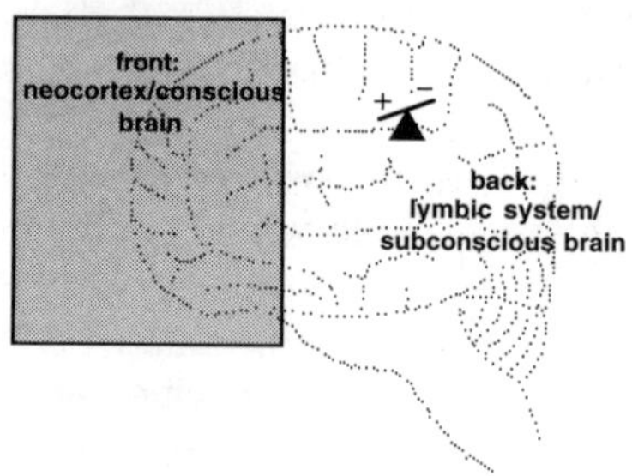

As the leader engages those whom they lead/manage/coach, the emotional variances of each generational segmentation must be understood and taken into consideration as coaching takes place.

How the *most senior member of the team one leads* internalizes things (thus how their emotions are stimulated and influenced internally and in turn what behavioral patterns are traditionally externalized), is radically different from how a *Baby Boomer* (and *echo Boomers,* those born within a few years after the Boomers that while they may be *Generation "X'ers"* demonstrate more of the *Baby Boomers,* behaviors and espouse more of their beliefs than that of their peers!) internalizes and externalizes. Conversely there are similar changes, differences and variations to generational segmentations for each of the subsets of *Generation "X'ers", Generation "Y'ers",* and *Mosaic/MTV'ers*.

Along with the generational segmentations each having variances in the types of emotions they have as part of the *apperceptive-mass* and demonstrate, each also has been conditioned by the generation as to how they are to share or express those emotions. Also, each generational segmentation was raised and conditioned with how the male and female are to demonstrate their emotions – and emotions have a direct correlation to the behaviors one exhibits.

As an example, with *older men (Centurion* and most *Baby Boomer* generational segmentations), they were raised/conditioned that emotions were to be kept internal and not shared externally. So emotions some times manifest as anger and rage and this would manifest in aggressive behavior. So the leader can quickly see and understand that the internal level of apperceptive-mass influences ones' emotions and those emotions directly influence the actions or reactions one demonstrates.

In coaching the emotional variances then, view each individual from the generational segmentation they represent and recognize how they have in turn been raised, conditioned and even expected to demonstrate their emotions – and what degrees of emotions are expected from a man versus a woman.

The coach may have to, as an example, move quickly to isolate an individual away from the team who is emotionally out-of-control by *"yelling, screaming, demanding, crying, etc."* so as to interact with that specific individually more effectively as the coach. By doing so, the leader can reduce (and potentially even eliminate) the negative influence upon others' *apperceptive-mass* on the team!

The coach may need to maintain conversational control by focusing individuals' attention and interest on issues which individuals may differ on, thereby keeping control of the potential negative emotions, which could otherwise cause a breakdown in communication among individuals and lead to the leader having a sensitive *dialogue* intervention with a more-firm coaching style of engagement with a specific individual.

The ability of the leader to coach the emotional variances effectively is again a hallmark trait of a successful coach of the future.

Building A Thriving Business

by Carl Potter

Building A Thriving Business

by Carl Potter

Do you really want a thriving business? Are you willing to spend the time to build your foundation for success? If you answered "yes" to these two questions, then the next step is to go to work.

Most people want to be successful, but not everyone is. What makes for success? Some use terms such as "habits," "foundations," "keys," "elements" or other descriptions. Whatever you want to call them, there are certain "things" required in order to be successful.

First of all, you need to be ambitious to be successful. You must *commit* to creating a thriving business, and you must *commit* to working hard. Without hard work, your business will never get off the ground. Success doesn't come from laziness.

Next, think about your *attitude*. Are you positive about what you're about to venture into? A positive attitude is essential because it will bring you through the times when problems occur and you get discouraged. Remember that success is never problem-free. Everyone makes mistakes, and things go wrong. You just have to be able to lift up your chin, learn from your mistakes and go on.

Now, if you believe you are committed to building a thriving business and know that you have the right attitude, there are several steps that you can follow to put yourself on the right track for success. These steps are the basis for the success I've had with my own thriving training and consulting business. My book, *Thriving Business* (Right Attitude Publishing, 2000) gives a thorough discussion of the following steps.

You must first learn to appreciate the industry you serve, then know whom you serve and what service you provide. You must also build and care for your network. I consider the most essential step to take is responsibility for what you do. The people in the industry you serve will appreciate you for it!

Appreciate the Industry You Serve

If you don't appreciate the industry you serve, others won't trust your advice. Those in your network need to know you are committed to making your industry the best it can be. Only then will they take your advice seriously.

Your attitude toward your industry is important. A proper attitude creates a desire to learn more about that industry. Attitudes are contagious. Others will pick up on your positive attitude, and it will spread amongst the people you work with and throughout your industry. A bad attitude is obvious and can really hold you back. Let me tell you about Bob.

While preparing the room for one of my two-day motivational seminars, Bob came up to me and introduced himself. He was wearing a black Harley Davidson cap and matching shirt. His hair was shoulder length and it kind of fuzzed out from under his cap. On top of that, he was wearing mirrored sunglasses and it wasn't exactly bright in the room! It wasn't hard to tell he was paranoid – his wallet had a heavy-duty chain attached to it that ran to his belt. I knew by his body language when he approached that he was looking for a conflict. I stuck out my hand and said "Howdy!" Without taking my hand he said, "My name's *Killer*, I don't have an attitude problem and I was made to be here!" Well, I said, "My name's Carl and I was made to be here, too!"

During the first day of the seminar "Killer" kept his sunglasses on and arms crossed. By mid-morning on the second day, he had taken his sunglasses off and relaxed. During a break he approached me and confided that he was having a pretty good time. "Killer" also admitted to me that he knew "this stuff," but thought his boss was the one that really needed to attend.

Later, I talked to "Killer's" boss about "Killer's" attitude. He said things were better, but said he thought "Killer" may need to attend the seminar three or four more times. Are you like "Killer?" Do the people you deal with see you as a candidate for my two-day motivational seminar? If so, my number is in the back of this book. Call me. You're welcome to attend our next seminar.

Many have an attitude problem because they focus only on their paycheck. Obviously, if none of us got paid we would probably not come to work. If all we look at is our paycheck, before long we will not like what we see. A person who is in a job or running a business for the money alone will never add value to the industry.

A person does not become more valuable without effort. Focusing on self-improvement results in personal development, which is the only true basis for career advancement and business growth.

Read the periodicals about your industry. Learn industry history. Discover why your industry came to exist. Talk to people who have been involved with the industry the longest. The more you know about the industry's history the more you can plan for its future. Become involved in the industry associations, and do what you can to help your industry succeed. In the 21st century, those desiring success in their careers and businesses must know their industry to be successful.

Look at the big picture. What industries do you think you're interested in serving? Think about your background for a moment. What have you done? What are you doing now? What do you know about the industries that strike your interest?

One phase of my career was spent as a recruiter for engineering personnel. During that particular phase, I learned the importance of being motivated to work for someone else. One of the first questions I would ask a potential candidate was "What industries would you like to work in?" The answer to that question told me where to start first. People have all sorts of different interests, likes and dislikes. You are probably the same way. It is important to know whom you serve.

Know Whom You Serve

If you don't know to whom your service is valuable, how do you know you provide a valuable service? Who is your "customer" or "client?"

No business survives without customers. In a corporate structure, job security comes from knowing that you have internal and external "customers" who rely on your service. In business it is the same way. Without customers or clients there is no business.

People who are successful in their corporate careers can tell you who their "customers" are. Successful performers know their audience.

Thriving businesses know who is benefiting from their services. The more you discover about whom you are serving the more likely you are to find ways to improve your service. Think about the companies that you might like to serve, and what services you can provide.

Know What Service You Provide

You need to nail down solutions you can provide to solve others' problems and how you can help them achieve their goals. Why should they hire you? What is it that will make them rave about the results you've provided?

My friend and networking partner, George Hendley, will tell you spontaneously what he does. His statement is that "I work with leaders who want to grow people." At *Potter and Associate, Inc.*, "we work with employers and associations that want to motivate their employees and members to peak performance." Both George and I have discovered that not being able to tell clients what we do will get us nowhere.

It has been said that you should be able to tell someone what you do in the time it takes to ride an elevator four stories. (Now this is not a SLOW elevator!) I call this the "elevator statement." As you develop your short, concise elevator statement, think about how you'll get the person to whom you're talking to ask, "so how do you do that?"

Be ready to tell everyone you meet your elevator statement. This means your mom, the postman, your friends and even the man on the street. Over time, you will refine your statement and will find that it comes naturally. You'll be surprised at how this simple statement will help you build your network. Others will be interested in what you do!

Build and Care for Your Network

Your network is the foundation of your business. And the success of your business will depend on the strength of the support network you build. Your support network should be made up of people whom you *admire* and with whom you are *connected.*

Connecting with someone means that you have a common value with him or her. It does not mean you agree with everything that person does. You may not like his style, but if it is effective, learn from him and respect him.

You need to build and nurture your personal support network. It is called a "network" not only because of its connecting parts, but also because of the ability of information to flow equally both ways. People who are a part of your support network will ask for your advice as much as you ask for theirs.

Network support is not a "one-way" street, or even a "two-way" thoroughfare. It's more like a junction of several interstate highways at a major interchange. In a network, ideas come and go in several directions.

When I first started my business, my wife Debbie would usually start the day off with, "What have you got going today?" I would say, "Oh, this and that." One day when she asked, I told her that I needed another client to fill my low points. Well, she threw cold water in my face (no, not literally!) and said, "Why don't you practice what you preach?" This made me mad! Not really mad, but it hurt because she was right! I was not making calls on people I knew. I was only wishing I had clients but doing nothing to move forward. I've learned that clients don't just show up on my door or dial my telephone number!

After my wife left for work and immediately after I finished pouting, I rolled my trusty Rolodex and went to work. My first call was to a friend whom I had known for some time. He asked me what I was up to and I said, "Oh, nothing. Just thought I'd call." We said our good-byes and hung up. It then occurred to me that I didn't ask him for anything. So I called another person I've known for some time. That call went much the same way as the first, but I asked if there was anything he needed and he said he didn't need anything at the time.

I didn't give up. My next call was to yet another person I had known for several years. This time my question was, "What's keeping you awake at night?" He told me about a project to develop customer service training for some field personnel. "Can I help?" We had a meeting, the project was scoped out and one of my best programs, *"Celebrating Quality Customer Service,"* was born. This project did wonders for my bank account. It's been said before, "You have not because you ask not." No kidding! You have to keep that network going.

Three keys to building and nurturing your support network are:

1. *Meet and talk* to everyone you can. Whenever possible, get a business card. Make contacts whenever the opportunity lends itself. Talk to everyone, everywhere you go, even at the grocery store and post office. You'll be surprised where leads will come from.

2. *Connect* with the people who appear to share your values. Find out if they actually do share your values. When you discover someone with whom you feel comfortable, ask to meet with that person. Remember to respect people's time. If you say you want to spend an hour with someone, don't take up more than an hour, and be on time.

Look for similarities in your products or services and ways that you can exchange ideas and resources to help each other to be successful.

3. *Nurture* your relationships within your personal support network. Find common ground with people. Always begin conversations with small talk. Let people know you are interested in them, not just their business. Find out about their hobbies and their families. Make them feel important. Take notes about them, so that you don't have problems recalling their family members' names. They'll appreciate your attention to detail.

The people with whom you network will probably become your friends. Respect their ideas and personal life. You don't have to go fishing or out to dinner with them to build a solid relationship. In fact, a work relationship can often work better than a close friendship. When working with people, be careful not to get too comfortable with them. You can relax, but always be professional.

Never *tell* a person in your network what you want. Ask! Too many people *take* from those willing to give until there is nothing left to *give*. Don't be a leech in your network. Ask people how you can help them. Use the old back-scratching method. If you scratch their backs, they're sure to scratch yours. Contribute from your knowledge and experience.

Your network is more than a list of names. It is easy to go through the company or association directory and pull out names. These names are like seeds that must be planted and cared for. Seeds can be planted, but unless they are watered and tended, they can die. Care for your network, and it can yield tremendous fruit.

Your network should be made up of *people you can count on* and people who can *count on you*. People will know they can count on you when you take responsibility for doing what you say you'll do.

Take Responsibility for What You Say You Will Do

Every successful person accepts responsibility. The hallmark of a successful person is someone who can be counted on to fulfill his or her responsibilities. It is vital to your success to follow through on your commitments. Don't let fear of failure stand in your way.

The fear of failure can destroy motivation and destroy what you're trying to accomplish. Aiming for success means being willing to take the risk to make a mistake and learn from that mistake.

Few highly innovative ideas or discoveries were done right the first time. Mistakes and discouragement are usually the first cities passed on the highway to success. Success usually comes after initial mistakes or discouragement.

If you take responsibility for your mistakes, others will more readily give you credit for your accomplishments. In building your network, look for the person who is willing to risk doing the difficult to accomplish the significant. When you find people who will take responsibility for their work, enlist them into your network.

The level of expectation of companies is often lowered to meet realities. For example, many supervisors are amazed when an employee regularly shows up for work on time. In some companies, people receive awards when they go a period of time without significantly injuring themselves.

While working in my corporate job of 17 years, I experienced responsibility in action. Those of us who were eligible were gathered up to be measured for jackets. The jackets were a reward for working safe without an accident for more than one year. Everyone was feeling good about the reward until Dennis, one of the electricians, said, "I don't want a jacket." He explained to us that he didn't see why we should receive something for working safe and not hurting others and ourselves. He claimed that we should be responsible enough not to get hurt in the first place. This was profound! What a concept! But I still wanted the jacket! Dennis made his point and elected to not receive his jacket. Me? Mine's hanging in my closet right now.

Arriving at work when you are supposed to show up and not killing yourself while you're there can earn you recognition! That is why in today's workforce it doesn't take much to stand heads above the rest.

Successful people would rather have five people on a project who will take responsibility than 50 slackers who don't know what the word "responsible" means.

I know this sounds a little too basic, but how do you like to work with people who are responsible? That's right! It's important to everyone. My clients are constantly on the lookout for this kind of individual. Companies want this characteristic in their contractors, parents want it in their kids, and everyone wants it in their friends. It is one of the most important ingredients for bottom-line success.

The Bottom Line

A thriving business is one that is built on relationships. You must know the industry you serve, know who you serve and what service you provide. Learn to build and care for your network. And, above all, take responsibility for doing what you say you'll do. If you combine these components with a commitment to succeed and a winning attitude, you'll be on the right track to building your own Thriving Business.

And That's The Truth! – or Understanding Ourselves And Finding The Real Truth

by Jack Pryor

And That's The Truth! – or Understanding Ourselves And Finding The Real Truth

by Jack Pryor

In 1983 there was a race in Australia from Sydney to Melbourne. The distance was about 875 kilometers. That equates to just over 543 miles. A race from one city to the other isn't new. In the United States alone there have been several auto races from one city to another. But this race was different. One of the differences, it was a footrace. A 543-mile footrace. Another thing that was different about this race was one of the participants, Cliff Young. Cliff was a local potato farmer and rancher and was not making a killing in the potato and cattle markets. He figured the prize money from the race was what he needed to get his life jump-started.

Now picture the day all the runners register for the race. Men have traveled from around the world to enter this race and there stands Cliff. Needless to say the media couldn't wait to interview Cliff to find out why he thought he could win a race like this. He would be competing against world class distance runners that had been training for months. Cliff had it all figured out. He explained that he raised cattle on his station and he didn't have a horse. In order to round up and work his cattle he chased them on foot. Since he had been chasing cattle since he was a young boy he thought he was in pretty good shape.

To enter a distance race takes a great degree of training and dedication. To enter a marathon requires a different level of training and dedication. Any race over 100 miles is considered a super marathon and this takes still another level of training, dedication, and support. To run 543 miles requires even more support. Think about it. You must have a place to sleep which requires a travel trailer or motor home. Running for several hours burns up a tremendous number of calories so you will probably have a nutritionist in order to maintain the high level of calories being burned. Some runners will have a pain specialist because you don't run 543 miles and not hurt. You will have a massage therapist so you can relax and your muscles can recover during your rest time. Cliff's crew consisted of his best friend, his sister, one of her girlfriends, and a couple of other friends.

Well, Cliff not only entered the race, he won the race, defeating the legends in distance running. He finished in 5 days, 15 hours, and 4 minutes. The second-place person was ten hours and more than fifty miles behind. One other thing unusual about this race is that Cliff was sixty-one years old when he set the new record.

How could a sixty-one-year old farmer beat world-class runners that had been training for months and years? At that time everyone knew that to run 875 kilometers you had to pace yourself. Everyone in the running world at that time knew the truth. And the truth was the only way you could go that distance was to run eighteen hours and sleep six. It had been determined by someone that six hours was the minimum amount of sleep you could get by with and still maintain strength and energy. All of the world-class runners knew each other and they all knew the truth. You could only run 18 hours and then you had to sleep 6.

The thing was, Cliff didn't know the truth. He didn't know you had to sleep. So while everyone else stopped to sleep, like the Energizer bunny, Cliff just kept going and going and going. Another truth was, to be a distance runner you had to pick your feet up and take a fairly long stride in order to develop a rhythm. Cliff didn't know the truth about distance running so he used a more efficient step. He picked his feet up just enough to clear the ground. He used a shuffle step.

After the race all the news media wanted to interview Cliff. They found out his diet was cold baked beans, spaghetti, and pumpkin juice. This started the greatest run on pumpkin and beans in the history of Australia. Everyone in the running world knew the truth. You had to run eighteen and sleep six and a human didn't have the ability to break that rule. Everyone thought Cliff won because of his diet. They didn't give him credit for breaking the rule. *Run eighteen, sleep six*.

I spent some time in the military and in the infantry we called Cliff's running style the airborne shuffle. I know for a fact you can go for miles and miles with that style of running. I also know you can go a long time without sleep. In one military activity we laid down (not in bed) and went to sleep on a Saturday night. We got up early on Sunday morning and started moving. We would stop occasionally for a rest. Sometimes we would stop and eat and other times we would eat on the move. We didn't lay back down and go to sleep until Friday. We were on the go for five days and nights. It's amazing what we can do when we set our mind to it. *Run eighteen, sleep six.*

How can a person go that long without complete rest and sleep? We were able to do it because we knew we could. We were good and we knew it. We didn't consider failure. We were efficacious. Efficacy is the power to produce effects or intended results. The ability to make things happen. When you put a group of efficacious people together, you form team efficacy and teams can accomplish tremendous tasks.

Our actions and thought processes aren't based on the truth, but rather on what we think the truth is. I was in the construction business for several years. I built new houses, remodeled houses, and consulted on new construction and remodels. When I started the remodel of our older farm house, I designed it so it would be comfortable and open. After the framing was completed I started placing the electrical boxes. Moving from the breakfast room to the utility room there is an ideal location for the utility room light switch on the left. Except the area is only wide enough for one switch box and the pantry light had to be located there. Since it wasn't wide enough for a double switch box I had to locate the utility room light switch on the wall to the right. This is the same direction the door swings and the switch would barely be behind the door's edge. Since that was my only option I decided we could live with that location.

About three years after the house was completed I was conducting a workshop on goal setting and I realized the real truth. The real truth was, since the area to the left wasn't wide enough for a double switch box I could have placed one box above the other or I could have used a single box and installed a double light switch that flips sideways. I was a professional carpenter. I had remodeled several homes. I had consulted with dozens of people. I knew the truth. I was so locked on to "it wouldn't work" I locked out all options. *Run eighteen, sleep six.*

If we can lock on and lock out on something as simple as a light switch what really important ideas are we locked onto?

When was the last time you made a decision based on the truth? And later found out what you thought was the truth wasn't. *Run eighteen, sleep six.* When was the last time you got upset about something or at someone because you knew the truth, then later found out you really didn't? *Run eighteen, sleep six.*

When we determine we know the truth we lock on to that truth and lock out everything else. We eliminate the possibility of finding the real truth. A question that we must continually ask ourselves is "What is the truth? Is this the truth or is it just my perception of the truth?"

When we are efficacious we truly believe there is nothing we can't do. When I spent five days and nights without sleep, I knew I was good. Our team was the best there was and we truly believed we were the best. We knew we would be able to accomplish any goal we were given. And we did.

A few years ago I found out I have a brain disorder. The good news is it isn't fatal. The bad news is I will always have it. Maybe the worst news is that you have it too. Lou Tice calls it LO/LO. Lock On Lock Out. I've added a third part. LO/LI/LO. When we know the truth and lock onto the truth we lock in to a narrow way of thinking (a box) and we lock out all options. *Run eighteen, sleep six*. Just like I locked onto "this space isn't wide enough for a double switch box." When we lock onto something like the light switch we develop a *scotoma*. A Greek word meaning "a dark area in the visual field or blind spot," a scotoma is an area we can't see mentally or physically.

Not only do individuals have scotomas, but organizations and industries have them. The architectural industry had a scotoma to what could be done to improve public restrooms. Think of the lines we still see outside women's restrooms, and not men's at conferences and public events. Since most architects were men, for years toilet facilities for women were not a major concern. Most women worked at home, and very few attended public events or conferences. The lines started forming as more and more women started working in the business world. Women need more time and more privacy than men. The architectural industry was "locked on" to how restrooms were built. And they "locked out" the idea of building larger or different facilities. Their first approach was to get women through the facility more quickly. They removed the bathroom counters so the women didn't have a place to put their purses. Since they wouldn't have a place for purses they would be less comfortable and would spend less time in the restroom. Next the coat hooks disappeared. Women had to pile their coats on top of the trash cans, but the rounded dome trash can tops stopped that. *Run eighteen, sleep six.*

Now the new convention centers are building restrooms with a men's door on one end and a women's door on the other with a moveable wall separating them. The rooms can be adjusted according to attendees.

RAS MA TAZ
or
HOW TO SEE WHAT'S IN FRONT OF YOU

The lower portion of the brain contains an area known as the Reticular Activating System (RAS). It controls the overall degree of alertness and keeps the brain ready for input. The RAS lets in data we value and anything that threatens us. The thalamus portion of the brain screens out insignificant signals and deals with movement. The thalamus and RAS work jointly in screening out and letting information in. If we weren't able to develop scotomas to some things, think how much information you would be bombarded with all the time. The ticking of your watch, every hair on your body, every blink, every swallow, every sound. Your brain would be trying to sort out all this different information constantly. There is research that indicates that Attention Deficit-Hyperactive Disorder is connected to the RAS. Thanks to the thalamus and RAS some of us can live our lives without this interference.

Tom Peters once said *"Perception is all there is."* It doesn't matter what the truth is, it's what people perceive as the truth. This statement is even more powerful when we realize how scotomas alter our perception. We act not according to the truth but to the truth as we perceive it to be. For fifty-one years the truth was I couldn't write. I don't know where it came from. I remember the fear and panic in elementary school, junior high and high school and even through graduate school when we had to write. I would pick up my pencil and my mind would go blank. I would have trouble thinking of my name much less something to write.

I developed a scotoma to writing. Then one day in Sunday School class we were discussing self-esteem. Each of us had to identify one thing we didn't like about ourselves. Well, guess what? Mine was that I couldn't write. After I gave my long explanation (excuse) of how I can't write, my wife said "He can write, you ought to hear the wonderful speeches he writes." I said "I don't write them, I mind map my ideas and just go with it." She said, "That's writing."

A few days after that, I pulled out my mind map of a two-hour workshop I had conducted and started writing. I was "locked on" to "I can't write." I "locked in" that other people could write and developed a scotoma to all possibilities. And I "locked out" the idea of just putting my speech/workshop on paper. Since writing a book was in my subconscious, the RAS allowed my brain to accept the input from my wife, "He can write, you ought to hear the wonderful speeches he writes." *Run eighteen, sleep six.*

I know some people that spend weeks shopping for Christmas presents. They will spend all day in a mall and go home and say, "I couldn't find a thing." When you go shopping and don't know what you are looking for, you won't find it. There is too much out there. You can't make a decision because there are too many choices. When my wife and I go shopping, we basically know what we are looking for before we leave the house. The first year using our RAS Christmas shopping took us two and one-half hours. Our record is one hour and forty-five minutes. We bought gifts for four parents, six brothers and sisters, seven nieces and nephews, one aunt, one secretary and three staff. That's an average of one present every 4.77 minutes. We didn't have the exact item picked out for each person before we started but we had our RAS open. When we walked into the first store in the mall, ideas started bombarding us.

The RAS lets you set the goal first and then figure out how to reach the goal. If you knew what to do to reach the goal, then it wouldn't be a goal. You would be doing it. First you figure out what you want and then the RAS makes you aware of all the data around you that will enable you to reach that goal.

There are two pictures of everything, the picture in your head (internal) and the picture of reality (external). Everything we do is based on a picture in our heads. We have a mental image of how we are, how we look, and how the world is. When we encounter something that is different from our mental picture, it creates some disharmony. This disharmony creates distress or eustress. Distress implies mental or physical strain that usually can be relieved. Eustress is the energy and desire we have to accomplish something.

I have a mental picture of my workbench being clean and all tools in their places. My life is no less hectic than yours so after a while my workbench starts getting cluttered. I will need to work on something and when finished, I throw the tools on the bench because I don't have time to put them away. After several days of this, the picture I have in my head and the picture of reality don't match. The difference in the two pictures creates eustress, the desire and drive to make the pictures match again. I find the time and energy to clean up and put everything away. I change the picture of reality to match the one in my head. We will do about anything to make the two pictures match. We will either change the internal picture or the external picture.

What is there in your life that is bothering you? The kitchen sink with its dishes, the laundry, ironing, the yard, the paint on the house, a project at work, or maybe it's that ratty old car you are having to drive.

A few years ago I decided to invest in precious metal. I made the decision to purchase a new Ford pickup. The Chevrolet Blazer I owned was paid for and not giving me any problems, but my internal picture was of me driving a new Ford F150 pickup. Every day I was less pleased with the Blazer. Finally I was so displeased I decided to go order my new truck. I was going to change the external picture to match the internal picture.

I went to the dealership to determine my options and place my order and was informed I couldn't order one because Ford was making a body style change. The new style would be ready in about three months. I looked at some photographs of the new style and thought it was the ugliest pickup I had ever seen. I went home very discouraged because the external picture of my new pickup didn't match the internal picture.

Later I picked up some promotional brochures and laid them beside my chair at home. Each evening that I could I would look at the new pickup and soon started thinking it didn't look too bad. By the time the new ones were at the dealerships I had decided they really looked pretty good. About two weeks of seeing new ones on the car lots and the streets I thought it was the best-looking pickup I had ever seen and I ordered mine. I changed the internal picture to match the external.

What do you really want to do but haven't tried because you don't know where to start? What goals have you not allowed yourself to have because you didn't know how to reach them? Where are you locking yourself in to thinking you can't? How are you locking out the answers? Start identifying those areas today. Let your RAS bring you the information you need. Start busting those scotomas, and lock on to a magnificent future!

Getting Good At Balance – Seven Strategies to Make Change Stick

by Mary Pryor

Getting Good At Balance – Seven Strategies to Make Change Stick

by Mary Pryor

The single greatest element of high energy living is balance; the greater the balance, the greater the joy, energy and creativity.
– Ann McGee-Cooper

Lasting change. Now there's an oxymoron. It's more than that though. Lasting change is also something that's necessary when things are out of balance. When stress is keeping you from functioning as you should, when you're unsure about the next decision, when you're confused about how to balance all the priorities in your life . . . it's time for a change.

Strategy 1-Get Unstuck

Just because change is necessary doesn't mean it's going to happen. True, a change might occur, but *lasting change* and balance in our lives is much harder to come by. That's true for four different reasons:

1. Because it's hard.
2. Because it takes work.
3. Because it requires commitment and a mind shift.
4. Because there is little or no immediate gratification with long-term change.

Remember that change is *your* choice. As W. Edwards Deming said, It is not necessary to change – survival is *not* mandatory.

Would you describe your life as a balancing act? The Life Balance Wheel is a great visual way to look at the balance in your life.

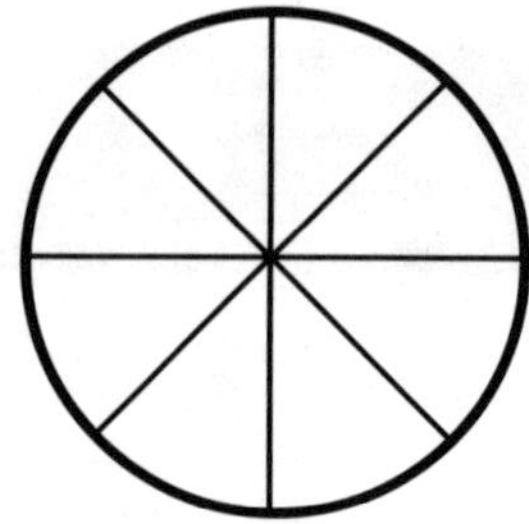

Think of the different roles you play, all those areas you need to balance. Each spoke of the Balance Wheel represents one of those roles — family, career, financial security, health, etc. You get the idea. For the one area in your life where you feel balanced, imagine that spoke reaching all the way to the rim of the wheel.

But the Wheel only reflects your balance if you draw each spoke *the length it is right now*. Been ignoring your health? The health spoke might not be as long as the one called career advancement. If it were a perfect stress-less world, all of your spokes and mine would reach to the rim. But some of your spokes — and mine — are shorter than that. Those areas are the ones crying out for a balancing act.

Sure, you can live with short spokes, but the wheel won't be balanced. If you plan to survive and thrive, it's important to unstick yourself from where you are right now. Mention change and you'll get a reaction. Mention change to me, suggest that there are lasting changes that would be beneficial to me, and you'll get a whole range of reactions.

Change is, to use a phrase popular with one of my colleagues, as old as dirt. And just like anything with a history, it's well established, not easy to fight against. Just think of how successfully you've been able to fight gravity in your life! Change is going to happen — either around you, or through you. The choice is yours. If you know, or sense, that change in some areas of your life, in your ways of doing things could make you much happier and more satisfied, start now by working on the short spokes. It's the only way to get unstuck.

Strategy 2-Check Your Assumptions

That's Ayn Rand's advice. Knowing your core beliefs about change is a key step in getting good at balance. Some people approach change with:

The Evolutionary Approach

Your basic assumption is that everything in life is a struggle. You see change as a defensive strategy against external hostile forces. This is the approach of choice for someone who might say, "You have to work so hard just to stay even in this industry." Taking the evolutionary approach, you're not even sure you can change. But if you can, and that's not a sure thing, you may be lucky enough to survive. This mind-set is based on just that — survival.

The Set In Stone Approach

Marked by rigidity and hard certainty, residents of Cement City will tell you "I can tell you from my experience, I've learned the only person I can trust is myself." Well, Rest in Peace. Because if you have all the answers and they all come from you, there's not much change on your horizon. All messengers will be shot. No doubts or fears allowed. Things will be done the same way, time after time after time. The problem with living in Cement City is rigidity. It causes organizations to die early; it causes dreams to die early too.

The "Others Know Best" Approach

No relation to the folks in Cement City, individuals here trust other people — exclusively. George Ray McEachern has a great philosophy about consultants and trusting the wisdom of others. Consultants, he says, will recommend what they know best and are comfortable with. There is no shortage of people who will be happy to tell you how to balance your life — based on their experience, not yours.

> Getting stuck in a particular way of understanding the world — whatever it is — is the cause of three major human diseases that I'd like to do something about. The first one is seriousness, as in "dead serious." If you decide that you want to do something, fine, but getting serious about it will only blind you and get in your way.
>
> Being right or certain is the second disease. Certainty is where people stop thinking and stop noticing. Any time you feel absolutely certain of something, you cease noticing other things.

The third disease is importance, and self-importance is the worst of all. As soon as one thing is "important," then other things aren't. These three diseases are the way most people get stuck.

Use Your Brain for a Change
– Richard Bandler

If you listen to Margaret J. Wheatley and Myron Kellner-Rogers' audiotape *A Simpler Way*, you'll hear them say that life leaps forward by two things — by the sharing of information and by linking together. Order and balance are free. We needn't struggle. We can even give up our belief that nothing happens without us.

Check your assumptions.

Check them now!

They may be keeping you off-balance.

Strategy 3-Take Down the Roadblocks

Two roadblocks may still be ahead of you. One is indecision. Expensive indecision. It's what's kept you exactly where you are right now. The other is that wonderful four-letter word FEAR. Either one of these roadblocks can stop you cold. And they do that every time you make a conscious choice to stay where you are and rationalize away a need for better balance in your life. Right at the roadblock, you'll hear people say,

"Well, now that I've had more time to think about it . . ."
"This really is not the best time for me . . ."
"I'm going to do this, just as soon as . . ."

But what each one of those means is, "Even though I don't think my life is balanced the way I'd like it to be, I'm too paralyzed to take the first step."

Fear and indecision are both powerful paralytic agents. They freeze your dreams and goals in place. They keep relationships just as they are. They can keep you indefinitely off-balance.

There are two ways you can make fear and indecision disappear. One is to simply choose to *do nothing differently*. That choice does have an effect on the balance of your life. It changes nothing, except it moves you backwards. Because while you choose to "leave things as they are" the rest of the world keeps moving. When you're facing the roadblocks and choosing to do nothing, you're operating with a Barrier Focus. The barriers are all you see. Be careful. As Lou Tice warns, you move toward the things you think about.

The other way to make fear and indecision disappear is tremendously powerful. More about that a little later.

Strategy 4-Stay in the Beanstalks

Think about this. Changing things for better balance in your life is your choice. You get to decide when and where and how the changes happen. Often when people are faced with change, they'll say, "I hate change!" when what they really hate is the imposition of change. Some of the most exciting changes you can make happen when you get to creatively decide how and what you want to change. And that requires staying in the beanstalks.

> **If you are going to kill giants, you must spend your time in the beanstalks, not in the pea vines.**

You cannot change if you stay where you are. What you accomplish in life is directly proportional to the time you spend in the beanstalks. If you spend your time and energy on small things, your results will stay small. You'll stay mired in the pea patch. Results may be immediate and easy to see, but they will still be small results – pea size.

And here's a helpful gardening tip:

Remember the physical properties of the pea plant. *Pea vines are elastic*. When you decide to spend time in the beanstalks, those vines sometimes snap you right back into the pea patch. They aren't called snap peas for nothing.

We do so much by habit. And behind every habit there's a belief – a reason for doing things that way. The older the habit the more entrenched it is. The more entrenched, the harder it may be to uncover the reasons for your behavior. I don't care about your habit of which foot gets the first sock in the morning. I'm concerned about habits that limit your potential.

If I'm in the habit of saying, *"Well, I could do that, but not just now . . . I really wouldn't know how to . . . I'd hate to rock the boat . . . I'm just not at that level . . ."* my belief is that there are no possibilities open to me at this moment. What you and I decide to notice blinds us to all other possibilities.

According to the Philosophy of Abundance, if you act as if there always will be enough, there always will be. This applies to money, time, resources, energy, everything. The opposite philosophy is the Poverty Mentality. Anytime you choose to say, "There's not enough . . ." (of whatever you think there's not enough of) there never will be! What's your philosophy? Think about it each time you hear yourself say, "There just isn't enough . . ."

Stay in those abundant beanstalks, because belief is the place from which true change develops.

Strategy 5-Big Frogs First

Mark Twain said, If you're going to eat frogs, it's best to eat the big frogs first. And our biggest frogs are our habits. Now I'd like to make this as tasty as possible, so for now, focus on which habits may be holding you in place — and keeping you from getting good at balance.

Often, important changes in life will require you to eat the big frog first. That big frog may come disguised as a huge first step, a serious commitment, something that requires planning or solitude. Frequently, we pass on this first course, by habit.

Interested in the nutritional benefits of eating big frogs first? By changing your priorities, you change your belief in what can be done — in a day, on a project, to improve a relationship, to further your career. And there's an extra health benefit! Not only is it nutritionally sound to eat the big frogs first, there's the added bonus of finding energy you may have lost. That energy returns when you choose to work on the major things that advance you toward your goals.

What you're actually doing is giving yourself permission to move ahead.

If you find it too distasteful to eat the big frogs first, there are other choices available to you:

- You can change your attitude about the "big" things you're not able to accomplish.
- You can change your focus – *away* from your dreams.
- You can change your attitude about growing.

There is usually a side dish here too – you can choose to hold on to the stress and tension that keep you from being balanced.

One last piece of advice from Mark Twain:

If you have to eat a frog, don't look at it too long.

Strategy 6-MOVE NOW! It Doesn't Have To Be Perfect

It doesn't have to be perfect.

It doesn't have to be good.

It just has to be.

Where and when did some of us get the idea that we can move ahead only when everything is in place? As Jim Stovall would tell you, all the lights do not have to be green.

You'd never stay parked anywhere in your car until you could see green lights in all directions. My guess is that you climb into your car, start it, take it out of park, (and here's the important part) YOU START MOVING FORWARD!

You know forward. According to Webster it means moving toward a point in front, onward, advancing. When you're parked, waiting for a better day, time, solution, idea – you put all your resources on hold. You tie up your feelings and resources because you're holding tight to, and not acting on, a solution that is "not good enough yet."

If you're prone to this red light thinking, the next time you're stopped at a mental red light, wondering, "Is this good enough?" ask yourself instead:

Is this a viable solution?

Is it something that would work?

See the difference? The key is to accept your pretty-good solution *that will work for now*. Focus on what's right, not on what's lacking.

Remember my earlier promise? The other, tremendously powerful way to make fear and indecision disappear? Here it is!

Any solution will access your resources and move you ahead.

Even if it's only a pretty-good one. It's only by accepting a solution, that your resources and emotions are freed up to DO SOMETHING! It's only by using your resources that you'll move closer to being balanced.

Try to remember that it doesn't have to be perfect or even good. It only has to be. The ideas you implement are the only ones that will move you ahead, while others wait for all the green lights and all the perfect solutions.

Do you know someone who is a born tinkerer? A person who can become totally involved with one question, one piece of machinery, one concept or challenge? A tinkerer keeps messing with things, and never feels "I've got to get this right the first time!" Actually, most tinkerers don't even think about "right" or "perfect." And no one ever told you and me that the main rule to live by is GET IT RIGHT OR DIE. Or even worse, GET IT RIGHT THE FIRST TIME OR DIE!

Children don't live by that rule. We don't tell them there's only one chance to learn to tie your shoes, ride a bike, master reading and writing. Missteps and mistakes happen in every learning process. When you build in fear of failure, you lock up your resources one more time.

Somehow the tinkerers of the world never got the Get It Right or Die message. They got the Find What Works message. Some of us need to tinker more, to stop waiting for the perfect answer, to begin working with what's in front of us, right now, even if it is only "pretty good."

If a cat spoke, it would say things like,
"Hey, I don't see the *problem* here."
– Roy Blount Jr.

Strategy 7-Proclaim a General Amnesty

I learned this technique from my friend Susan. Susan walked into work one morning telling us she had proclaimed amnesty on all the undeveloped film in her kitchen drawer. That meant, she explained, that every reason she had in the past for not developing all that film did not count during the Amnesty Period.

Susan had already developed the first rolls of film and had spread them out to look at the prints. She was trying to remember exactly what, when, and where was happening in those photos. One set, she finally decided, was her daughter Stacie's first day at kindergarten. It took her a while to figure this out however, since Stacie is now 14 years old! I think those pictures mean even more to Susan at this time than they might have 13-14 years ago.

The important point here isn't that Susan FINALLY got those pictures developed. The importance lies in what she did:

She gave herself a period of time

- free of guilt
- free of past behavior
- free of clutter

Amnesty works because it involves a behavior change. The nicest part about Susan's amnesty program is just that—it involved doing something differently, and it worked!

Proclaiming General Amnesty works on all sorts of things—unfinished manuscripts, unmet commitments to relatives and friends, long unkept promises to yourself.

Baseball pitcher Tom Seaver once asked manager Yogi Berra,

"What time is it?"

Berra replied, "You mean now?"

Although it sounds grammatically incorrect, here's another quote from George Ray McEachern: *"Nothing is."* There is nothing to tie you to outdated habits, beliefs, or systems. Unless you choose otherwise.

"We must not be misled to our own detriment to assume that the untried machine can displace the proved and tried horse."

– Major General John K. Herr, 1938
U.S. Army

"The energy produced by the breaking down of the atom is a very poor kind of thing. Anyone who expects a source of power from the transformation of these atoms is talking moonshine."

– Ernest Rutherford, *physicist*
Circa 1930

"Fooling around with alternating currents is just a waste of time. Nobody will use it, ever. It's too dangerous . . . it could kill a man as quick as a bolt of lightning. Direct current is safe."

– Thomas Edison, *inventor*
Circa 1880

At least 80% of the information you need to make decisions is already stored in your brain. So when it comes to getting good at the balance in your life, you've got the data to work with.

All change happens in how we see ourselves, how we handle information, and how we treat each other.

Today is all the tomorrow there is.

Teams: Connecting With Something Larger Than Ourselves

by Kent Rader

Teams: Connecting With Something Larger Than Ourselves

by Kent Rader

Beginning in the 1980's, the landscape of American business began to change. In response to reductions in revenue and the ever increasing expense of doing business, layoffs and downsizing became commonplace. The workplace was being asked to do more with fewer resources. The development of teams to accomplish specific goals was one response to this new business environment. Also, developing well-functioning organizations became more important to doing more with less. In both cases, the qualities of a well-functioning team became essential to successful businesses.

Teams are defined as "a number of persons associated together in work or activity," as with a sports team. This chapter will discuss the dynamics of winning teams in the context of two successful organizations. The first is the Chicago Bulls under the direction of Phil Jackson, the second is Southwest Airlines. Both have reached the pinnacle of their respective worlds and have done it in remarkably similar fashion!

Phil Jackson in his book, *Sacred Hoops, Spiritual Lessons of a Hardwood Warrior* stated his main job as a basketball coach was to awaken the spirit of the players, reconnecting them with their love and joy of playing the game. This allows players to "blend together effortlessly." Jackson goes on to succinctly state the problems with most teams when he says,

> "It's often an uphill fight. The ego-driven culture of basketball, and society in general, militates against cultivating this kind of selfless action, even for members of a team whose success as individuals is tied directly to the group performance. Our society places such a high premium on individual achievement, it's easy for players to get blinded by their own self-importance and lose a sense of interconnectedness, the essence of teamwork."

The purpose of this chapter is to better equip managers and executives to develop and direct quality, winning teams. Two areas of winning or quality teams will be examined here. These are as follows:

1. A shared or common vision or goal that is owned by the members of the team.

2. An environment that is conducive to creativity by the members of the team.

Let's get started.

SHARED OR COMMON GOAL

Before a team can become successful, it must first agree upon a shared vision or common goal. This may not only be one of the most difficult tasks associated with a quality team, but also one of the most important. Phil Jackson states, "This is the struggle every leader faces: how to get members of the team who are driven by the quest for individual glory to give themselves over wholeheartedly to the group effort. In other words, how to teach them selflessness." To do this the members of the team must take ownership in a common goal. Sports teams have a common goal or a shared vision, the winning of a championship, but in business this is sometimes more difficult to determine.

We will discuss three distinct phases of developing and adapting a common or shared goal. These are as follows:

1. Development of a goal for the team or organization.

2. Communicating this goal to the members of the team or organization.

3. Assigning the tasks to the members of the team to achieve this goal.

Development of a Common Goal

The first task for leaders of an organization or a team is the development of this vision or goal that will drive all decisions of the group. This is not a formal mission statement, but the actual reasons for being in business or why the team is in place. What does the group want to accomplish? What is its purpose for existence? Why did the members come together as a group?

Southwest Airlines is one of the best examples of a team with a vision and has achieved remarkable success by following it regardless of what others in their industry have decided to do. Kevin and Jackie Freiberg stated in their book *Nuts* that it was determined from the beginning of this maverick of the airline industry that it would be a company built on developing a specific market niche. Southwest Airlines would be a low-fare, short-haul, point-to-point carrier. Their original cities of Dallas, San Antonio and Houston upheld this vision.

In 1978 the airline industry was deregulated and Southwest Airlines had to make some decisions. Howard Putnam, the president and C.E.O. in 1978 asked senior officials to a conference to determine how they would proceed in the environment of deregulation. He said, "We aren't going to leave this room until we can write up on the wall, in a hundred words or less, what we are going to be when we grow up!" After two days of deliberation, the group decided they would stick with the formula they had employed since the beginning. They would remain a low-fare, short-haul, point-to-point carrier and that has continued to be the strategy for over twenty years.

Putnam says, "Most companies fail in their growth because they don't have a vision. They don't know where to go. When you have a vision and someone comes to you with some convoluted idea, you can hold it up to the vision and ask, 'Does it fit? Does it fly? If not, don't bother me.' A vision must be so strong that it can outweigh the egos of managers that might want to take off in a different direction."

This is the same idea stated by Coach Jackson earlier in this chapter. When he took over the Chicago Bulls, his first step was to visualize what the team would be under his tenure. He stated, "My vision could be lofty, I reminded myself, but it couldn't be a pipe dream. I had to take into account not only what I wanted to achieve, but how I was going to get there." Jackson wanted to build the Bulls into a championship team and wanted to utilize certain aspects of basketball that he had learned as a player and a minor league coach. Mainly the selflessness necessary for teamwork. He formulated a strategy that he could share with his team. Later when decisions needed to be made, just as with Southwest Airlines, they would be done in context with Coach Jackson's vision of the team.

The first step for leaders of a team or organization is to determine a mission or goal for the group. Visualize what the team will accomplish.

- Is it redesigning of a work process to make it more efficient?
- Is it to improve the quality of the company's product?
- Is it to improve customer satisfaction via improved service?
- Is it to do more work with fewer resources?

This goal is what will drive decisions in the future in order to make the organization successful.

When I organized my company, Competitive Advantage, I developed what my vision of the organization would be. I wanted to work with organizations who wanted to increase profits through the development of happier, healthier employees! I saw my company developing programs and resources that would help employees with stress reduction, developing healthier lifestyles and assisting leaders of organizations to develop environments more conducive to satisfied employees. This is what drives my actions on a daily basis, just as with Southwest Airlines or Phil Jackson's Chicago Bulls!

Communication of the Goal

The second task for the leadership of an organization is to communicate the team goal, enabling members to begin taking ownership of this goal. Phil Jackson said he set up the principles of the system he was going to follow, the famous triangle offense and getting all the members of the team involved in the games. He stated, though he set up a vision for his team, *"Visions are never the sole property of one man or one woman. Before a vision can become reality, it must be owned by every single member of the group."*

Jackson began this process of ownership by communicating his vision with the two leaders of the team, Michael Jordan and Bill Cartwright. These communications included "What's in it for me" because when a member's needs are met by the vision, ownership of the goal begins.

Michael Jordan had individual success, but no N.B.A. championships to go along with it. He long held a reputation for being competitive and Jackson understood how much it meant to Jordan to add a championship crown to his resume. Phil Jackson's system was designed around getting everyone on the team involved in the game. This meant that Michael Jordan would have to take less of a role in this new team, not more! Coach Jackson was nervous when he discussed this with Jordan, but said it went better than he expected. Michael Jordan began to accept Jackson's vision of the team because the "What's in it for me?" was an opportunity to win a championship!

Jackson knew Bill Cartwright was a leader, not so much on the floor like Jordan, but in the locker room. He wanted Cartwright's endorsement of the vision because he knew Bill could communicate this to the other members of the team in the confines of the locker room. Bill's experience with other championship teams had already taught him the importance of a common goal and he bought the concept immediately. Being asked to share leadership of a team that had previously been led by the incomparable Michael Jordan fed his need of being influential.

Phil Jackson didn't stop communicating this vision after these initial conferences, but continued on a daily basis until the team took ownership of this system as their own.

Southwest Airlines' goals are communicated to all employees all the time. One strategy discussed in *Nuts* is that managers of Southwest Airlines communicate, communicate and communicate some more. The Freibergs state,

> "One of the reasons Southwest has been so successful in getting people to internalize and embrace the company's principles and priorities is consistent communication. Rather than having the mission statement in one place — the lobby — Southwest displays it everywhere in the system to serve as a performance standard and a constant reminder of what is important for *all* employees."

When a team member knows the goal and understands the positive effects of achieving it, that team member will begin to take ownership in the goal.

Assigning Tasks to the Team Members to Achieve the Goal

Having communicated the team's goal and having secured personal acceptance of it, the next ingredient for a winning team is members accepting responsibility for the tasks necessary to achieve the goal. Ownership of the goal will assist in keeping employees focused on the relevance of tasks. In the beginning, before complete ownership has been accepted by the members, it may be essential for the team leaders to assign tasks to individual members. In assigning tasks, the leader of the organization will want to take into consideration the strengths and weaknesses of the individuals in the organization. Coach Jackson stated in *Sacred Hoops*,

> "Just as fish don't fly and elephants don't play rock and roll, you can't expect a team to perform in a way that's out of tune with its basic abilities. Though the eagle may soar and fly close to the heavens, its view of the earth is broad and unclouded. In other words, you can dream all you want, but, bottom line, you've got to work with what you've got. Otherwise, you're wasting your time.
> The team won't buy your plan and everyone — most of all you — will end up frustrated and disappointed. But when your vision is based on a clear-sighted, realistic assessment of your resources, alchemy often mysteriously occurs and a team transforms into a force greater than the sum of its individual talents."

He developed principles for the team members and communicated them daily to the players. He said, "The principles serve as a mirror that shows each player how well they're doing with respect to the team mission." The players of the Chicago Bulls knew their role on the team, the tasks that Coach Jackson asked them to perform, and how their task would contribute to the overall goal of the team.

As team members accept ownership of goals and begin to understand their role in them, they begin to develop what Jackson calls, "group intelligence." Once a group begins to develop this intelligence, it must be allowed flexibility to be independent of supervisors or leaders. This group intelligence further instills ownership of the goal by the members of the group and transforms them into a team!

Phil Jackson discussed this with regard to the triangle offense.

> "Once the players have mastered the system, a powerful group intelligence emerges that is greater than the coach's ideas or those of any individual on the team. When a team reaches that state, the coach can step back and let the game itself 'motivate' the players. You don't have to give them any 'win one for the Gipper' pep talks; you just have to turn them loose and let them immerse themselves in the action."

It is the same with the members of a business team or organization.

Southwest Airlines is a great example of group intelligence and leadership that empowers team members to take ownership of goals. *Nuts* points out that the whole business outline of the airline, including "systems, structures, policies, procedures and practices of the organization are designed and lived out so that employees genuinely feel that they come first." Employees are asked to make decisions on what they believe is best for the organization and the independence given by management allows them to do this.

The book is filled with numerous examples of employees acting in ways they believe to be right. For example, taking stranded customers home with them or committing company resources to help customers when necessary. Southwest Airlines, through the development and communication of a common goal, as well as employee understanding of a personal role in this vision, has developed a tremendous group intelligence. Management has allowed group intelligence to continue to grow unencumbered by dictates of leaders. Their success is attributed greatly to the employees delivering unprecedented service to airline passengers.

When individuals take ownership of a goal, they think of their tasks with a different perspective. They take personal responsibility for the success of the team or company. If they are allowed flexibility by the leaders of the organization, the members of the team begin, according to Coach Jackson, to "immerse themselves in the action" of the team. Team members with ownership in the goal and a group intelligence don't need an inordinate quantity of rules to follow or to be supervised heavily because his or her actions will be in accordance with the goal.

It is well known that when individuals feel involved, they care more about the outcome of the organization. In the book *Healing the Downsized Organization* Delorese Ambrose, Ed.D. discusses that motivational theorists like David McClelland have outlined three needs associated with motivation in work situation. These are as follows:

1. The need for achievement;
2. the need for affiliation;
3. the need for power.

These needs are met by organizations or teams with members who share ownership in the goal of the team, understand their role in this goal, and are allowed the flexibility to develop that "group intelligence."

To summarize, members of organizations or teams must take ownership in a common or shared goal in order to be successful. The leadership must determine what the vision of the organization or team will be. Once determined, it must communicate this common goal to the members of the team so ownership can begin to be taken. This communication must be constant and consistent until ownership of the goal is firmly imbedded in team members. The tasks necessary to accomplish the goal must be assigned to the members of the team based on individual strengths and the leadership of the team must allow members the flexibility to develop their own "group intelligence." This freedom further allows the members of the team to accept ownership in the goal. Once the team members take ownership in the shared or common goal, their actions will be determined by the goal, not undue supervision or rules.

With the team or organization having developed a common goal, let's move to developing an environment that is conducive to a successful team.

ENVIRONMENT

Today's business world is fraught with distrust, stress, lack of loyalty, diminished morale, and little creativity! Much of this can be attributed to the environment in which we conduct our organizations. Healing the Downsized Organization discusses the effects of downsizing on the survivors of the organization. Many of the negative aspects of today's business world can be attributed to the aftereffects of downsizing. These negative aspects have led to poor quality of products and service, dissatisfied customers, and continued shortsightedness of companies at the expense of long-term benefits.

It is my experience, as well as the experience of many successful organizations, that there are specific environmental factors that contribute to the success of a team and the extinction of negative aspects, even in difficult business environments. These include an environment of trust built on the twin pillars of honesty and integrity by management, humor, and an atmosphere which allows for the making of mistakes. When these factors are in place, not only will an organization have happier, healthier employees, but employees exhibit more creative problem solving skills which leads to more successful products and greater customer satisfaction.

A Trusting Environment Built upon Honesty and Integrity

Though it should be assumed that honesty and integrity are present in the environment of all businesses, they are too often not! Dishonesty and lack of integrity lead to distrust between members of the team and management. Distrust facilitates the erosion of morale and creativity, as well as increasing stress. Let's discuss these pillars of trust separately.

Frank J. Navran states in his book, *Trust and Trust: The First Two Victims of Downsizing,*

> "There are no exceptions, no justifications and no rationalizations which suffice to deviate from the position that employees are always entitled to the truth. The fundamental basis of trust in an organization is truth telling. *You are your employees' best source for honest, accurate and timely information.* The truth is the first essential building block, the foundation, of a trust-based working relationship."

Ambrose further points out studies done by James Kouzes and Barry Posner which state the number one expectation of members of an organization is that the leaders will be honest with them. Members of an organization or a team that is experiencing distrust are more concerned with protecting themselves than achieving a common goal.

In the book *Running Within*, Jerry Lynch and Warren Scott define integrity as, "the constant and consistent refusal to compromise your talents, abilities and sense of self." I would say it is also doing what you say you will do. As so often is stated, people with integrity "walk the walk"! This is the second building block of trust. Doing what you tell others you will do, as well as doing the right thing by constantly refusing to compromise your sense of self will lead others to know they can rely on your words to flow into actions which are consistent with these words.

The benefits of trust built upon the twin foundations of honesty and integrity is exemplified by Southwest Airlines' relations with their unions. In *Nuts* Kevin and Jackie Freiberg state they believe that the honesty and integrity of the management of Southwest Airlines has had long-term benefits for the airline. They wrote,

> "Trust is fed by personal integrity. Trust grows when we keep our promises and follow through on our commitments. You have to be deadly earnest, completely authentic, and do what you say you are going to do to earn people's trust. When people know they can count on you, your words and actions have more power to influence them. This is why Herb Kelleher and Southwest Airlines have had such successful union relationships. Kelleher is a man of his word. He thinks straight and he talks straight, so people respect and trust him."

In January 1995 the pilots reached a ten-year work contract with the airline. Not only is the term of this agreement unheard of, the fact that the pilots agreed to freeze their wages in return for stock options for the first five years was equally unheralded. Much of this result can be attributed to the trust the pilots had in management or they would not have been willing to commit to such a long-term agreement.

Another story in *Nuts* that demonstrates the benefits of trust and integrity is as follows.

> "Rod Jones, a former union representative, remembers that when he first arrived at Southwest his union's board of directors was in the final phase of establishing a contract with the company. The package had been approved, except for one item. The union had a pilot whom they thought the

company had treated unfairly. Board members wanted his matter taken care of before they recommended the contract to the pilot group."

"At dinner on the evening of the board meeting, Kelleher and John Schnobrich, president of the union at the time, discussed the issue over drinks. When the board reconvened the next morning, Schnobrich indicated that the issue had been resolved."

Jones recounted that when he asked how it had been taken care of, Schnobrich stated, "Herb told me it would be taken care of." When Jones asked if this was in writing, he said Schnobrich stated in an irritable fashion, "You don't need it in writing. When Herb Kelleher tells you something is going to be taken care of, it's take care of." Further Schnobrich stated, "Herb gave me his word on it and that's better than any piece of paper!"

One of the most trustworthy individuals I have ever known is our son Keith. He has long been honest and seems to follow his conscience with regard to making decisions within his life. If asked when he learned the importance of telling the truth, I'm sure he would tell you it was from the famous, "pork chop" incident, as it has become known around our house.

Keith inherited his mom's prolonged eating habits. (Her mom used to clean a lady's house in their hometown of Lincoln, Missouri, if the lady would reciprocate the favor by feeding Twyla because it was such an exasperating experience!) Once when Keith was three, we had pork chops for supper. When we were finished with dinner, Keith had barely made a dent in his meal, so Twyla and I began to clean the dishes and kitchen. Soon we heard Keith's request to be excused from the table, indicating he had finished with his meal. Upon checking his progress, we discovered no pork chops on his plate, so he was excused.

When we picked up his plate to finish our task of cleaning, much to our chagrin, we discovered the pork chops we had cut up for our innocent son hidden under the lip of the plate. We got quite a laugh from the thought process that must have gone on in his mind! ("Hey, I'm onto something here. I can put these under this plate and they will see my plate is clean! It will take them years to find them and by that time I will be long gone! Maybe they will even think it is Maggie by that time!) Needless to say, Keith had quite a different reaction when we asked him about this and decided his punishment for lying would be to retire to bed immediately. I can still hear his gentle sobbing in my memory from that night. He long remembered the lesson of honesty from that same night. I wished all of us learned this lesson as easily as this young man I continue to admire today!

Humor

Humor is the ability to experience joy even in the midst of difficulties, serious business situations, and even the unstable environment so often experienced in today's business world. There are numerous studies supporting the positive emotional and physical benefits of using humor. One of the first was chronicled by Norman Cousins in his book *Anatomy of An Illness*. Cousins was stricken with a serious collagen illness. He understood that there were negative physical changes due to negative emotions, such as stress, so he wondered if there wouldn't be positive physical changes due to positive emotions, such as laughter. With this thought, he began to include humor in his therapy, joyously finding that ten minutes of good belly laughter had an anesthetic effect and would give him two to three hours of pain-free sleep!

Other studies on the positive influences of humor include:

- Dr. Burk, Loma Linda University School of Medicine produced carefully controlled studies showing that laughter lowers serum cortisol levels and increases the number of active lymphocytes. Both stimulate the body's immune system, physically counteracting the effects of stress.

- The book *Stress Without Distress* by Hans Selye says that stress is dependent on the perception of events, as well as our thinking. Humor gives us a different perspective on our problems.

- Patty Wotten, R.N. did a study on 231 American nurses and found that when encouraged and guided to use humor, they felt they gained control over their lives. External events can not be controlled, but we can exercise control over how these events are perceived and the emotional response to them.

Southwest Airlines has built much of their business around the positive effects of humor in the workplace. The Freibergs state in their book that Southwest takes fun very seriously and hires people accordingly.

> "The company's recruiting and hiring practices are built on the idea that humor can help people thrive during change, remain creative under pressure, work more effectively, play more enthusiastically and stay healthier in the process."

The airline hires people for attitude and trains for skill!

Phil Jackson learned about the power of humor from a Bull's assistant coach, Johnny Bach. Because of the inordinate amount of time players reviewed game films, Bach would insert scenes from movies to lighten the mood of the players. Jackson occasionally included clips of *"The Wizard of Oz"* in these. The players found them funny and as the mood lightened, they began to learn more from the mistakes they were making in the games. They became a teaching device for Jackson, as well as a source of humor.

I find in my own business that some of the most enjoyable times are when I share a good laugh! Mona, a part-time employee at my company Competitive Advantage, has a reputation for having a great sense of humor. She and I find similar experiences funny and seem to have the ability to put a funny spin on the mundane. She can't wait for me to return from my speaking engagements with my latest story about something entertaining that happened along the way. Usually in the midst of these experiences there is little to find funny, but in retrospect a humorous spin can be put on it and we get a good laugh. I also make prank calls to her using voices of characters around our small, Oklahoma town when we are not together in the office, just for a laugh. (If you see me in your local airport on my cell phone talking with a funny voice, you can bet it is Mona on the other end of the call!) I often comment to my wife that I love having Mona in the office because it makes work so much fun!

Humor can offer members of an organization or team the ability to have a different perspective on events of the group! It not only has positive physical and emotional effects on the employees, it can make coming to work an enjoyable experience rather than "a job" that must be endured for eight hours at a time! It also has a tremendous influence in building a team. When people laugh together, they feel closer because of this common, fun experience.

Allowing People to Make Mistakes

Robert Kennedy once said, "Good judgement is the result of experience. Experience is the result of bad judgement." Without the ability to make mistakes, people will not be inclined to take risks and chances.

Phil Jackson states in *Sacred Hoops* that, "At the core of my vision was getting the players to think more for themselves. Doug Collins (The former Bulls' coach) had kept the younger players, especially Scottie Pippen and Horace Grant, on a tight rein, frequently yelling at them when they made mistakes. Throughout the game they'd look over at the bench, nervously trying to read his mind. When they started doing that with me, I immediately cut them off 'Why are you looking at me?' I'd ask. 'You already know you made a mistake.'

This freedom to make mistakes and learn from them allowed these players to learn the new system installed by Jackson. As they learned the triangle offense, they became more confident in their decision-making. That would not have happened if Jackson had not given them permission to make mistakes.

Southwest Airlines has removed the fear of failure by not rejecting employees who reach high and fail. This encouragement and the rewarding of the small successes, regardless of the failures, has fostered an environment that encourages risk taking to achieve success!

There are stories like Matt Buckley and his idea of RUSH PLUS. Though he thought his idea would revolutionize the shipping industry by offering same day delivery of products, the idea bombed miserably. Matt stated his failure was painful and he not only avoided his peers, including Mr. Kelleher, at the Southwest corporate offices, he was concerned with losing his job! Not only did he not lose his job, he found his peers were supportive in helping him heal from the failure. They reiterated that it was alright to make mistakes because that was how we learn! Thomas Edison, when asked about all of his failures in producing the electric lightbulb, retaliated that he hadn't failed, he had found thousands of ways not to make an electric lightbulb.

A few years ago my daughter Maggie wanted to be in a school talent show. She was in the second grade and was going to sing a Reba song in front of not only her peers, but the high school students. I feared for days for her because I wondered what would happen if she failed! I worried she would be hurt, she would be upset, she would never recover from a public humiliation! When she was met with enthusiastic applause I must admit that I had a tear in my eye and learned a valuable lesson. She was only going to grow by taking risks that challenged her and that meant that she had to be open to failure.

Failure is a wonderful learning tool and only comes when we take risk. Lois Creamer, a marketing person who works with speakers in building their business, told me once that if you don't ask the question, the answer is always going to be no! If risks are never taken, the organization will never challenge itself and the desired success will never be achieved.

An environment of honesty and integrity that encourages finding the humorous side of situations, and allows members the freedom to make mistakes by striving to achieve new goals, is an environment abundant with creativity. Creativity is the ability to develop new ideas, as well as utilize old ideas in new ways. This is one of the most important ingredients missing in today's business world. New product lines, more efficient ways of doing business, improvements in customer service are all dependent upon creativity.

In his book *Slowing Down to The Speed of Life*, Richard Carlson discusses creativity in what he labels free-flowing thought. He states this creative mode of thought is stress free, nonfatiguing, enjoyable and natural.

Carlson points out during a recent survey people were asked where and when they get their most creative, best ideas. The top three answers were the shower, while on vacation, and driving the car. What do all three of these environments have in common? The environment is relaxed and not filled with pressure to come up with an answer to the problem. For organizations to thrive in today's world economy, creativity is essential and it will only blossom in a relaxing environment. The essentials for this environment are honest and trustworthy leadership, one that allows the funny side of the daily situations to be enjoyed, and one where mistakes are tolerated in the spirit of learning.

One of the best stories of creativity is told by Jim Fay of the Love and Logic Institute in Colorado. He is in the business of consulting with educational organizations. One day he received a call from a principal of a junior high in Kansas with a terrible problem! The principal said the 7th and 8th-grade girls had discovered makeup. Mr. Fay asked why this was such a problem? The principal said, "You don't understand. They have discovered lipstick and in between classes, they put it on in the bathrooms and then put their lips to the mirror and kiss it, leaving lipstick all over the girls' bathroom mirrors!" Mr. Fay didn't understand why this was such a problem, but he continued with the conversation. He asked the principal what he had tried to stop this crisis? The principal said he had tried everything! He had banned makeup from the school, met with all the female students, even called parents, but nothing seemed to deter this behavior. Jim admitted he didn't have an answer, but agreed to travel there to see what he could do.

Mr. Fay arrived on Monday morning. As he walked down the hall discussing the problem with the principal, a small woman approached the two, saying she was the new janitor and she thought she could help with this situation. Mr. Fay said, "Well it is worth a try!" He thought it would be better if one of the team members solved the problem instead of relying on an outsider. The janitor said she would try her solution during the first class break that morning.

During the first class break, the junior high girls were in the bathroom putting on their makeup, including the lipstick that was causing such a controversy. The janitor walked in with a mop and proceeded to enter one of the stalls. As she entered the stall, she lifted the seat with her foot, pushed the mop into the toilet water and began to scrub down the mirror with the toilet water! Jim Fay states that not only did this cause a cessation of the lipstick marks on the mirror, three of the girls instantly puked!

The creativity of the janitor helped the principal in eliminating a discipline problem. Even though the janitor's duties didn't include dealing with discipline problems, she was a member of the team with ownership in the school's goal of educating students. Creativity can help organizations be successful in today's competitive business world, but it must be incubated in an environment of trust, humor and one which allows mistakes to be made when attempting new heights.

I want to close by wishing you the best in all your endeavors and reminding you that our actions have consequences that, in the words of Sylvia Boorstein, "echo way beyond what we can imagine!" May your actions always be right!

Valentine's Day Every Day

by R. Michael "Mike" Ruckel

Valentine's Day Every Day

by R. Michael "Mike" Ruckel

Every February 14th we celebrate Valentine's Day. We rush around buying greeting cards, candy, and flowers for our girl friends, boy friends, wives, husbands, families and friends to tell them just how much we love them. What if we made everyday Valentine's Day!

Everyday a Valentine's Day! I think this is an exciting idea, don't you? Rather than just telling our family, friends and loved ones how we love them let's include everyone. How do we do that? We simply extend our love to everyone. We don't have to say, "I love you" to everyone. We can show them with a kind word. What if we can say something warm, friendly and nice to the person at the grocery store checkout, the person who cuts our hair, to our fellow employees? How about being a good neighbor? Maybe we could pick up trash or leaves in the neighbor's yard just next to our yard as we clean our own yard. We can show our love through our actions. I know a person who did just that and made everyday a Valentine's Day for those around him.

His name was Mr. Rob (not his real name) and he owned a hearing aid business in Amarillo, Texas. I did not see Mr. Rob very often; you see he was in his 70's or 80's and some days were good days and some days were not so good. His assistant Pat took care of the business most of the time. However, on this beautiful, bright sunshiny January afternoon when I walked into Mr. Rob's business, Mr. Rob was there and he was having a good day. We talked a little about business. However, we spent the afternoon talking about the power of love and then went to dinner and continued to talk about the power of love in action until nine o'clock that evening. Mr. Rob told me about some of his experiences in his life and how he loved life and those around him.

LOVE FOR HIS CLIENTS AND BUSINESS

Mr. Rob understood the fear and anxiety of a person with a hearing problem. To reduce the fear and make them feel comfortable he made his place of business like his home, a very nice home. His office had very fine furniture in it. Not office furniture but very nice home furniture. There were nice leather sofas and chairs, quality wooden tables and beautiful lamps to make his office like a home to anyone. He offered good books and magazines to read. The lighting was warm and cozy. Off to one side there was a hospitality room like a small kitchen. Mr. Rob provided soft drinks, coffee, tea or hot chocolate along with several kinds of cookies for his clients to make them feel at home. You see Mr. Rob knew that if his clients were comfortable and relaxed the fear would pass and they would feel good about the process of hearing again. Loving his clients, making them feel good first. Love made his business a success.

LOVE FOR HIS EMPLOYEES

Next he told me about Pat and when she had come to work for him some 10 or more years before. Her husband had died from alcoholism and this work was something new for her. Mr. Rob took away her doubt and fears about being able to do the job and told her just how easy it would be as he trained her in this new career. On her first payday Mr. Rob took her to the bank and had her open two accounts. One was a checking account and the other was a savings account. He said that she should put 10 percent of each check into her savings each payday and if she did he would match it. Then he proceeded to train Pat in the hearing aid business. He sent her to some of the finest audiology schools and the schools put on by the manufacturers of hearing devices. She became very good and began to run the business for Mr. Rob.

About two years before the time we spoke, Mr. Rob hired another young lady, Karen, to work with Pat and he gave her the same benefits he had given Pat. Pat had remarried and Karen was already married. Both became pregnant about the same time and they delivered their babies within a week or two of each other. This was just two and a half months before my visit on this beautiful day. Doctors have encouraged new mothers to breast-feed their babies for the good of the baby and the mother. This was the case for both Pat and Karen. However, Mr. Rob said, "this is not going to work out. You young ladies are going to have to have baby sitters. You will have to make sure your babies are fed properly and you may have to leave work to do this. This is not the best situation for you or your babies. So we will create a nursery here in the office for your babies."

That afternoon when I walked into their office there was a desk to the left of the door and behind it was a baby bed. Straight across from the door and to the right was another desk and behind it was a baby bed. There was a grandmother sitting next to one of desks holding one of the babies loving it and talking to it while she was there for her hearing needs. This was truly a wonderful sight and it felt good. It was the power of love in action.

Mr. Rob was concerned about the well-being of his young ladies and did not want them eating in the fast food restaurants around the office. He told me that he would prepare gourmet lunches at his home and have the ladies and their babies come out to his house to eat there. Then he knew that they were eating healthily. When the weather was cold and rainy or snowy he would put the food into thermal containers and take it to the office and they would eat there. Mr. Rob did not want the babies out in the cold. He was concerned for their health.

Mr. Rob said he calls down to the office two or three times a day to find out just how things are going. To make sure that Pat and Karen were okay and if they need any help or if there is anything they might need. He told me he ends each phone conversation with "I Love You." One day Pat asked "Mr. Rob what do you mean when you say 'I Love You,'" and he said, "I am wishing you success, happiness, joy, peace, prosperity and good in your life." Truly making each day for his employees a Valentine's Day.

LOVE FOR OTHERS

Being aware of others and how they help and contribute to the good of the community is another way Mr. Rob expressed love on an everyday basis. He told me while living in California some years before, he took notice of the telephone. He said to himself, "What a wonderful instrument the telephone is and what good service I receive." So he sat down and wrote to the President of Pacific Bell and told him what a wonderful instrument the telephone was and how he loved the wonderful job his employees were doing and he thanked the President of Pacific Bell for the good service. A few days later the President of Pacific Bell called and thanked Mr. Rob for his letter of praise. He said "I am posting copies of your letter in all Pacific Bell locations so the employees will know that there is someone who loves and appreciates what they do. They don't often get letters of praise. However, they get a lot of letters of people complaining about their service." Here is a person who took the time to reach out to others with a word of praise showing how he loved what they were doing. How many times have we thought about sitting down and writing someone and telling him or her what a good job they were doing? Then we forget to write the letter or note. A letter or note with a compliment could make the day a Valentine's Day for someone.

Isn't it interesting that two grown men could sit for almost six hours and talk about the aspects of love and how it can make a difference in the various facets of life? The stories that Mr. Rob shared with me were wonderful. My experience with this remarkable person I felt should be shared with you.

WHAT I LEARNED

I learned a lot from Mr. Rob on this beautiful day in January. I learned that if you want to be successful all you have to do is love life and everything in it. I thought if I could just improve by 10 percent using what I learned from this man my life would improve greatly. I remembered the old saying "You can catch more flies with honey than with vinegar" and that's true. So I started a campaign to be a better person and go out and win more friends. What I learned was to smile more, to say more kind words, to be helpful, to go a second or third mile, to praise more, to exercise more patience, to look for the good in everyone and everything, and there is good in everyone. We may just have to look for it.

With my family and friends I work hard to support and praise their ideas, goals, decisions and the way they want to live their lives. If I keep my mouth shut and give them support they will find a way to succeed. Like the bumblebee who doesn't know that aerodynamically he can't fly, and flies anyway. Even today I still have a long way to go. This process is ongoing, but it works. How?

As a sales person I stopped selling and started winning friends and I have sold more. You see people buy from people not companies. People will buy from people they know before they buy from a stranger. First of all they will buy from a friend that they know and trust. This is what I did only some of before I met Mr. Rob. I am doing more of it now. It works! Loving life does bring success. Mr. Rob's life was built on making friends in all areas of his life and loving them.

Here is a poem I think describes Mr. Rob's way of life. It is from *Unity* magazine, Unity Village, Missouri, and written by Viola L. Lukawiecki.

L O V E

Love enough and love will give you wings; It will cushion the rough places in your road, easing the strains, straightening the way before you, making effortless the tasks, erasing the drudgery, replacing it with pleasantness.

Refuse to harbor any feeling other than love. Your body cannot be out of ease, that is — diseased, while love fills your mind and heart.

You will be fearless — for perfect love casts out fear.

You will be happy — for inharmony cannot enter where love is.

You will become beloved — for like attracts like, and love is the greatest attracting power.

You will never be lonely — for love peoples your world with loving companions.

You will never be sad — for love is the greatest happiness-maker.

You will be alive, alert, aware — for love sharpens all faculties.

You will be successful — for love never fails.

Love with every ounce of your energy, and no other task will be required of you.

Fill your mind and heart with love — to overflowing — and life will pour its richest blessings upon you!

HOW CAN WE MAKE EACH DAY A VALENTINE'S DAY?

It's simple, all we need to do is to start LOOKING WITH EYES OF LOVE, LISTENING WITH EARS OF LOVE, THINKING THOUGHTS OF LOVE AND SPEAKING WORDS OF LOVE and we too can transform each day into a Valentine's Day. David, a former member of my Toastmasters Club and a friend would say, "I Love It" when anything was said or done (right or wrong). I thought, what a great affirmation to use in any situation. So I started to use it too. It does make a difference!

So when a customer apologizes for causing a problem, I say "I Love Problems to Solve." Customers and their problems are not an inconvenience, they are why I Love Selling.

You and I can start today making everyday a Valentine's Day. We can extend more love to our families and friends. Then we can reach out to our fellow employees, the people we do business with and to everyone around us, looking for the good and praising it. This is what my friend Mr. Rob did and he experienced success in all areas of his life.

Making Lives A Success!

by Mike Seikel

Making Lives A Success!

by Mike Seikel

"Success" humor: A man knelt and prayed aloud, "Lord, make me successful and please keep me humble." His wife knelt beside him and prayed, "Lord, you make him successful, I'll keep him humble."

Some years ago I was a program coordinator at the Oklahoma City office of the Federal Bureau of Investigation (FBI). A young lady, half my age, worked for me and we became friends. One day she asked, "Mike, what makes you so successful?" The question came as a surprise. I had never really thought of myself as being particularly successful. When I asked why she thought I was "so successful," she said something like, "you have a good career and are respected by your coworkers; you have a wonderful family and you are a good husband and father; and I know you have a deep faith in God. You should think of yourself as being successful."

After I thought about her question, I told her about an experience I had as a student at the University of Oklahoma (OU). An acquaintance and I were talking about our goals in life. Actually, he was talking about his goals . . . I didn't have goals. Vaguely I knew I wanted to be a U.S. Marine Officer and a Special Agent with the FBI. At that time, however, the only thing I was really concerned about was passing an upcoming test. He said his life goals were, *"to spend his life developing a close relationship with God, to have a family he could be proud of and to be the kind of husband and father his family would be proud of, and to have a career that would support his family comfortably and would make a contribution to the society."* I wish I knew who he was so I could give him credit. He was just a guy I worked with at a student cafeteria. I do know that he made me think and he stimulated me to put direction and meaning in my life. *I recognized that to be successful I had to be successful personally, professionally and spiritually.* I adopted his life goals as my life goals, too. I was confident he wouldn't mind sharing.

The young coworker said the story gave her much to think about and her question about my successes gave me much to think about. I was nearing retirement from the FBI and I began to look back on my life. I spent quite a bit of time looking at my successes and, yes, my failures. I found that it is very difficult to look at your own life objectively. In fact, I believe it is impossible but you can look at your life more objectively than you usually do. When you do that, you learn some things. The philosopher's advice, *"Know Thyself,"* is good advice and looking back on your life as objectively as you can is a good way to get to know yourself. It can be rewarding, but it can be disappointing, too!

After spending some time looking back on my successes and failures, I developed **"A Formula For Success!"** Notice I didn't say *"The"* formula for success. I used *"A"* because I recognize that other people have ideas about success and theirs may be as valuable, or more valuable, than mine.

My formula for success is:

(Experience + Growth + Self-discipline) x Positive Attitude = Success!
Your life goals and the formula you develop may be different and that's okay. We all have to define "success" for ourselves. After defining "success," we have to work at achieving it ourselves, in our own way. No one can define it for us, or achieve it for us. My idea of "success" was pretty well defined by me when I adopted the fellow student's life goals. I began to work toward those life goals and life became a joy.

Let me tell you a little about my formula.

(Experience + Growth + Self-discipline) x Positive Attitude = Success!
(<u>Experience</u>: "Experience really is the best teacher!" It is important that we learn from our experiences and the experiences of others . . . famous people and not so famous people like our friends, relatives and coworkers.

A little "learning from experience" humor: The first time you visit a farm you learn from experience: when you walk in a cow pasture you watch where you step! It always amazes me to see people making the same mistakes over and over. I do it too, but not like some people I have observed. Remember this old saying? "If you always do what you've always done, you will always get what you always got." Poor grammar, but it makes the point. As I looked at what I had "learned from my experiences," I got to "Know Myself" better. I had known for years that I am basically shy and that I lack self-confidence. Looking at myself more objectively than I ever had before, I admitted to myself that I am a "lazy procrastinator of average intelligence and little self-discipline who tends to go in many different directions rather than stay focused on a few things." Also, I lack "self-confidence." (Didn't I tell you that getting to "Know Thyself" can be disappointing?) When I admit this about myself, I can work to overcome the shortcomings, laziness, procrastination, and lack of self-discipline, focus and self-confidence. I learned some other things, too, but this is intended to be an essay, not a book of many volumes!

I have also learned much from other people. I make it a point to look at the lives of famous people and learn from them, and I learn from the lives of friends, relatives and coworkers whom I admire, and from the lives of some I don't admire. People will observe someone making a mistake and experience negative consequences then make the same mistake and experience the same negative consequences. Amazing!

Something else I have learned from experience is to set written goals, short-and long-term. People who have written goals accomplish many more of their goals than people without written goals. Consider **S.M.A.R.T.** goals, goals that are **Specific, Measurable, Attainable, Realistic**, and **have Target dates.**

It is never too late to learn from our experiences and to learn from the experiences of others. Learning from experience can improve our lives personally, professionally and spiritually.

(Experience + Growth + Self-discipline) x Positive Attitude = Success!
+ Growth: "Change is inevitable; growth is optional!" It seems like the longer I live the faster things change. It is human nature to resist change, yet things are going to change and there is nothing we can do about it. *Resisting change leads to frustration; accepting change and growing with change leads to satisfaction. Sometimes we can even influence change to be a positive rather than a negative.*

A little "growth" humor: Children learn much and "grow" by discovery. When our granddaughter, Lisa, was six years old her grandmother gave her a youth dictionary.

Lisa immediately sat down and began looking at it. She looked at a word and picture on the first page and said "A, apple." She turned a page or two, looked at a word and picture and said, "B, boy." Turning another page or two, she looked at a word and picture and said, "C, cat. Hey, this dictionary is in alphabetical order!"

I was not a good student in high school or the first time I was in college. In 1960, I graduated from OU with a bachelor of business administration degree. Later I went to school part-time and earned two more degrees: a bachelor's degree in religious studies from Loyola Marymount University in Los Angeles, and a master's degree in criminal justice from the University of Central Oklahoma (UCO) in Edmond. I was a much better student at Loyola and UCO. I was interested in the subjects and I was growing. In fairness I have to mention that I was a better student at OU after I married my wife, Rosalie, during my junior year. Rosalie has always been a positive influence on me and I hope I have on her. We have supported each other in our various endeavors and *"personal, professional and spiritual growth has always been an important part of our lives."* We have worked together to develop our religious beliefs, to raise a good family and to pursue noteworthy careers. We are both active Christians. I was a career husband, father and F.B.I. Special Agent and Rosalie was a career wife, mother, middle-school teacher and school counselor.

Reading and writing are great ways to grow. I believe we learn more when we "read" than when we "watch" or "listen." When we watch something, television, videos, movies, we are relatively passive and someone else is forming the pictures for us. When we listen to something, cassettes, lectures, seminars, we can be relatively passive and often we tend not to put much effort into listening. When we read we are usually a more-active participant. We form our own mental images and we remember and relate to our own mental images better than we do to those someone forms for us as on television or in videos. When we read, we "listen" to ourselves even though we may not read out loud. Basically, when we "read" we are "watching," "listening" and "actively reading," especially if we underline, highlight, look up word meanings and reread to ensure understanding.

When we write, we think more about what we are saying and we organize our thoughts. We read what we have written and we consider what we are saying from a more objective point of view than when we are talking or thinking without writing. We also find the "holes" in our thinking and, if we really want to grow, we do some research and "fill those holes." I have written much. I haven't published much, but I have written much . . . and I have learned much from what I have written.

As I have gotten older I have found that I can't do the physical things I once did. Some things I can't do at all anymore; others I can't do as well. Aging and limitations can be frustrating, but I have found other ways to grow, particularly reading and speaking professionally, to find satisfaction. Yes, *change is inevitable; growth is optional*. It is never too late to grow personally, professionally and spiritually.

(Experience + Growth + Self-discipline) x Positive Attitude = Success!
+ Self-discipline): "Our degree of success depends on our degree of self-discipline!" There were thirty seconds left in a professional football game. It was fourth down and the team with the ball was behind by two points. If they didn't get a first down on this play they would lose the game. The quarterback threw a pass but it was too high. The receiver was out of bounds and the ball was five yards over his head. Still, a defender tackled him. An official blew his whistle, threw his yellow flag and shouted "penalty!" The penalty gave the losing team a first down and another opportunity to win the game. I don't recall who won and it doesn't matter. What is important is what the color commentator said: "That defender should never have tackled him. He is supposed to be a professional and that is a lack of self-discipline. Football is like life, *your degree of success depends on your degree of self-discipline."* I don't believe a truer statement was ever made. **Your degree of success in anything depends on your degree of self-discipline**.

I have heard people complain about their "bad luck," or blame "other people" or "circumstances" for their lack of success in an endeavor or activity. On several occasions I have discussed their "bad luck" or their "circumstances" or the alleged influence of "other people" and almost always it has been the person's own fault that they weren't successful. They didn't prepare; they were late; they were inattentive; they procrastinated; they depended on someone else; they did a poor job; or, something else happened that was within their control but they lacked the self-discipline to control it.

Often I ask my seminar attendees to raise their hand if they have gone to hear one of the popular motivational speakers. A number of hands go up. Then I ask, "How many of you have obtained the speaker's material? His or her books, tapes, videos, and have used the material so that you are thoroughly familiar with it and have put it into practice in your lives?" Rarely does a hand go up. Then we talk about self-discipline!

We talk about things like this: it takes time, self-discipline and a desire (making it a priority) to change habits, break bad or inappropriate habits and establish new habits. Some habits take much longer than others to break or establish. Smoking and alcohol are among the toughest. Here is a good example: several years ago my thumb and index finger on my left hand were becoming numb. The doctor told me to begin wearing my watch on my right wrist, that the watchband was too tight on the left wrist and was causing nerve damage. My left wrist was a little larger than my right wrist. It took ten months to establish the habit of putting my watch on my right wrist each morning without thinking about it. (Several months after wearing my watch on the right wrist regularly, the feeling came back in my left thumb and forefinger.)

One reason we have so much trouble dieting, or exercising regularly, or breaking bad habits and establishing new habits is that we often don't make it a priority and use self-discipline to "change our behavior" over a long enough period of time. I have heard that it takes at least twenty-one repetitions, or twenty-one days, to change the simplest habit. More difficult habits take longer, sometimes much longer. Although I haven't found any scientific studies reflecting this, it is noteworthy that advertisers often ask us to use their product "for thirty days" and then return it if we are not satisfied. They expect that after thirty days using their product will become a "habit."

All of us can benefit from putting a little more self-discipline in our lives. Is it too late for a little "self-discipline" humor? Of course not. Actually, this is a little "lack of self-discipline" humor: The great baseball manager, Casey Stengel, was asked if he had made a decision. His response, "I made my mind up, but I made it up both ways."

(Experience + Growth + Self-discipline) x Positive Attitude = Success!
X Positive Attitude: "A positive attitude creates opportunity; a negative attitude ruins lives!" Attitude really is everything! I believe to be successful personally, professionally and spiritually, I must add experience, growth and self-discipline and then multiply them times a positive attitude.

A little "attitude" humor: Casey Stengel is credited with this one, too: "The secret of managing is to keep the guys who hate you away from the guys who are undecided."

Answer this question for me: **Why do you have more opportunity to succeed than anyone in the world . . . in fact, than anyone in the history of the world?** *(The answer will be given at the end of this essay.)*

There are a number of things to think about when you think about attitude. For one thing, research tells us that when we are happy, when we feel good about our accomplishments and ourselves, when we do things that make us feel proud, our brains emit chemicals. Some are called "opioid peptides" or "endorphins," short for "endogenous morphines." ("A Pleasure Chemistry," Psychology Today, July/August, 1988.) These chemicals can have a positive effect on our physical and emotional health. I suspect that the converse is true: when we do things that make us feel depressed, feel bad, that make us feel ashamed, it is detrimental to our physical and emotional health. Attitude! The choice is yours.

Enthusiasm is contagious. "People who like others are people others like." It's good to associate with people who have "contagious enthusiasm for life." We will be more positive about our lives. "Successful people associate with successful people." Successful people ask the advice of others: a form of teamwork. Remember, "Teamwork makes the dream work."

"Encourage vs. discourage." Remember to encourage your children and not to discourage them. **Research tells us that on the average, 78 percent of the influences on us during our most formative years, age 0-5, are negative influences** (Resource Associates Corporation, Reading, PA, 1998). "No, no Johnny." "You are not old enough to do that." "Children should be seen and not heard." "Stay out of that." "Leave that alone." "Don't break that." "Don't talk to strangers." "You just wait until we get home, young man!" And it goes on and on. We spend the rest of our lives fighting those negative influences.

Take control of your life instead of letting life (and other people) control you. Make positive choices. When you have a choice to make, ask yourself, "How will this affect me personally, professionally and spiritually?"

Look for opportunities to turn negatives into positives. To do that you have to control your anger and frustration and consider all your options. Often you have to swallow your pride and admit you were wrong, or ask for advice.

To varying degrees we all have a need to "care for" and "share with" others. Meet that need and you will feel more "positive" and better about "you."

Pick positive role models.

Select the reason/s that can keep you from succeeding:

Lack of education/talent ___ Age ___

Handicap or disease ___ Race/Sex ___

Lack of opportunity or time ___ Other ___

Death ___ You ___

As far as I am concerned, the only things that can keep me from succeeding are "death" and "me." I believe the same is true of you, too. (In fact, I expect to succeed after death, if I am successful spiritually.) Notice I even put "Other" so you can make up any *excuse* you want for not succeeding.

No matter how good life is, it can always be better. *Do you need to fine-tune, adjust or change your attitude?*

Speaking of questions, here is the answer to the question I asked earlier: *you have more opportunity to succeed than anyone in the world, in fact, in the history of the world, because you live in America! Let's quit taking our country for granted and take advantage of the opportunities.*

I challenge you for the next thirty days to review your life and learn from your experiences; to study and observe people you admire and learn from their lives and experiences; to grow personally, professionally and spiritually; to put more self-discipline in your life; and to fine-tune, adjust or change your attitude to a more positive attitude.

You do this for thirty days and it will change your life.

I wish you God's blessings and every success.

Yes You Can!

by Jim Stovall

Yes You Can!

by Jim Stovall

It was one of those rarely precious places and times when the whole world stands still long enough to review your past, experience your present, and get just a glimpse of your future.

I was standing backstage in a huge arena. In just a few moments, I knew I would be introduced, and I would walk onstage and spend an hour with thousands of people—sharing with them my innermost fears and triumphs along with my perspective on the world. As always, I was experiencing a flood of emotions, ranging from terror—knowing that I was expected to entertain and motivate thousands of people—to gratitude—feeling thankful for the fact that I have the privilege of pursuing my passion and really making a difference in people's lives.

Then I heard the music start. It signaled the time for my presentation to begin. A deep, professional voice boomed out across the vast arena, introducing me, and I listened to the now-familiar introduction.

"Ladies and gentlemen, Jim Stovall has been a national champion Olympic weightlifter, a successful investment broker and entrepreneur. He is Co-Founder and President of the Narrative Television Network, which makes movies and television accessible for our nation's 13 million blind and visually impaired people and their families. Although originally designed for the blind and visually impaired, over 60 percent of NTN's nationwide audience is made up of fully sighted people who simply enjoy the programming.

"Jim Stovall hosts the Network's talk show, *NTN Showcase*. His guests have included Katharine Hepburn, Jack Lemmon, Carol Channing, Steve Allen, and Eddie Albert, as well as many others. The Narrative Television Network has received an Emmy Award and an International Film and Video Award among its many industry honors.

"NTN has grown to include over 1,200 cable systems and broadcast stations, reaching over 35 million homes in the United States, and NTN is shown in 11 foreign countries. NTN programming is also presented via the Internet at NarrativeTV.com, serving millions of people around the world.

"Jim Stovall joined the ranks of Walt Disney, Orson Welles, and four United States presidents when he was selected as one of the 'Ten Outstanding Young Americans' by the U.S. Junior Chamber of Commerce. He has appeared on *Good Morning America* and CNN, and has been featured in *Reader's Digest, TV Guide*, and *Time* magazine. He is a successful author and columnist. The President's Committee on Equal Opportunity selected Jim Stovall as the 1997 Entrepreneur of the Year.

"Ladies and gentlemen, please welcome Jim Stovall."

As I walked onto the stage, I could feel as much as hear the thunderous applause. I calmly went through my normal routine as the applause continued. I walked forward and found the front of the stage by placing my foot on the very edge. I counted my steps just as I had done earlier in the day when I spent 45 minutes pacing back and forth across the platform while the arena was still empty.

As a totally blind person, I am forced to create my own little world before I am able to meet a huge audience in their world.

As the applause died down, I felt comfortable in my surroundings, and I knew where I was on that stage as well as where I was in the world. I began sharing my story, and—as always—I am still amazed how I went from there to here.

I remember a time in my life when I had not yet learned any of the principles that I now have the privilege of sharing with people around the world.

At its core, the process of learning and teaching are one in the same. When you learn something, you have impacted only yourself. When you teach it, you have impacted a handful of people. But, when you teach people to teach, you can change the world.

When I was seventeen years old, I was preparing to go to college.

I remember having to fill out a voluminous application that included a physical exam form. Part of the physical exam paperwork required me to get a routine eye test. I remember going to our family eye doctor and having him take me through the normal routine. He put drops in my eyes and examined them with a very bright light. Then, he had me read an eye chart across the room.

Just as I thought he was about done, and I was ready to leave, a second doctor entered and performed the same ritual. Finally, a third doctor came in and ran several other tests.

Eventually, all three doctors met with me in a conference room and shared with me the message that would change my life. "We're not sure why, and we're not sure when, but we do know that some day you will be totally blind, and there's nothing we can do about it."

My whole world stopped at that moment. I was in shock. The only way I could deal with the situation was to deny the reality. So, that fall, I went on to college simply pretending I had never heard those fateful words.

Near the university I attended is a school for blind children, and I'm not sure if my motives were to learn more about blindness, make some kind of bargain with God, or just to help out, but in any event, I went to the school for blind children and met the principal. I told her that I was a college freshman, and I had no background, training, or experience working with blind children, and I would like to teach in her school. You can imagine how excited she was to see me! But, she was a kind soul and told me that if I really wanted to, they had one child I could work with one-on-one.

I agreed and asked her what it was I would teach this child in our one-on-one sessions. She explained that Christopher was four years old, was totally blind, and had many other physical problems. She went on to explain that they had done many tests, and they had determined that Christopher would never develop or advance any more than he already had. And what they wanted me to do was keep him quiet and keep him away from the other kids so they could learn their lessons.

As I look back on it today, I realize that Christopher was suffering from the most severe disability of all—that is being faced with no expectations.

We always live up to the expectations that we have of ourselves or those expectations that we allow other people to place upon us.

They had no expectations for Christopher, and the only training they gave me were two very simple things. First, they instructed me to keep his shoes tied, as they were afraid he would trip and fall because he had never learned to tie his shoelaces. Secondly, they told me I had to keep him away from the stairs because he had never learned to climb the stairs, and they were afraid he would fall down the staircase.

Other than those two things, they really didn't care what I did as long as I kept Christopher quiet so that the other students could learn their lessons.

That first day, I was introduced to Christopher and immediately noticed that he was much smaller than you would expect a four-year-old child to be. He was totally blind and had many other physical problems.

He and I sat down and had a serious conversation, and I told him, "Young man, before I leave here, no matter how many weeks or months or years it takes, you are at least going to learn how to tie your shoes and climb the stairs."

And he replied, "No, I can't."

And I responded, "Yes, you can."

And he replied, "No, I can't."

And I responded, "Yes, you can."

And he replied, "No, I can't . . ."

If you have ever spent any length of time with a four-year-old child, you know that they can argue all day long.

Christopher and I began working every day, learning how to tie his shoes and climb the stairs. Meanwhile, I was attending the university, and my eyesight was fading quickly. When it got difficult, I simply prepared to quit.

Quitting becomes a habit, just as perseverance becomes a habit. So, after several weeks of the school year, I had reached what I thought was my breaking point and resigned myself to dropping out.

I went to the school for blind children for what I thought would be my last day. I met with the principal and told her that because of my own visual impairment I was going to drop out of college, so I wouldn't be able to come here and work with Christopher any more because I simply couldn't make it.

I didn't realize that Christopher had been dropped off early that morning, and he was standing outside the open door to the office, hearing our entire conversation. So, as I went out to tell him goodbye and tell him that I loved him and tell him that I hoped that someday someone else would show up and spend some time with him, he turned to me and repeated my own words back at me by saying, "Yes, you can!"

And I replied, "No, I can't."

And he persisted, "Yes you can!"

And as I replied, "No, I can't" once again, I was mentally preparing an explanation so I could justify to Christopher how my challenges were somehow different or greater than his were. But, before I could begin my weak explanation, it hit me like a ton of bricks. The obvious answer was, "Stovall, either get up and do something with your life, or quit lying to this poor kid in telling him he can do things in his life."

Three years later, I graduated from that university with honors. And the same week, I had the privilege of my life with what little vision I had left, to observe then-seven-year-old Christopher climb three flights of stairs, turn and sit on the top step, and tie both of his shoes. Since that time, I have interviewed some of the greatest people of the 20th century either on television, for my books, or for newspaper columns. While the superstars from sports, politics, movies, and television have all had their impact on me, no one has ever impacted my life as did Christopher.

He taught me the pure, unadulterated wisdom of the ages which is, quite simply, no matter what your goal or the obstacle you're facing, the answer is always, "Yes, you can!" The dream would not have been put inside of you if you did not have the capacity to achieve it.

So the question is never "Can we?" The question is quite simply, "Will we?" When we realize that the dream has been put inside of us because we have the capacity to achieve it, and all of the provisions necessary for our success are in place, anything less than our ultimate destiny becomes unthinkable.

I have the privilege of sharing Christopher's story and his message with millions of people around the world on a regular basis. On each such occasion, I enter into a partnership with the individual members of the audience. As you read this book, I want to become your partner in your own success.

Any time that you believe that your success is too far away or somehow the elements are not in place for you to achieve your ultimate destiny, I want you to pick up the nearest telephone and dial 918-627-1000. That is the main number of the Narrative Television Network. We have people who answer the phone 24-hours-a-day, 7-days-a-week, and they know there is one kind of call that I will always return. You simply tell them that Jim Stovall told you your dreams could come true, and right now, you're not sure.

I will always call you back, because I want you to know that from this day forward you have one person who believes in you and believes in your dream. If you don't think so, simply pick up the nearest phone, and call me.

I am looking forward to your success and for you to be able to live out your destiny.

About The Authors

Dawn L. Billings, M.A., LPC (M.O.M.) and Corbin Billings, K.I.D.

Dawn Billings is founder of Beyond Empowerment, a Tulsa-based company dedicated to ending violence in schools. Dawn travels nationally speaking on leadership, violence prevention, character education and how to develop greatness in children.

Dawn has a Master's degree in Clinical Psychology and is the director for Lifebreak Counseling Center. As a licensed professional counselor, Dawn has been in private practice for ten years, working with individuals, couples and families.

She is the author of *Greatness & Children: Learn the Rules*, and coauthor with her eleven-year-old son Corbin, of *The ABC's of Becoming Great, The ABC's of Peace and Compassion, The ABC's of Great Leadership*, and a companion workbook *Choose To be Great.*

Corbin Billings is 11. He is a sixth grade student in Tulsa. He won the JC Penny Volunteer of the Year award for his region this year. Corbin is an author, a professional speaker, environmental advocate, tree of life ambassador and the youngest member to meet all professional requirements in the history of the National Speakers Association. Corbin was selected as a *Millennium Dreamer* by McDonald's, Disney and the United Nations Educational Scientific Cultural Organization. He was flown to Disney World to be awarded and recognized in May 2000.

Dawn and Corbin travel nationally and encourage thousands of people yearly to live their dreams.

Dawn L. Billings, M.A., LPC
Corbin Billing, K.I.D.
5512 South Lewis Avenue
Tulsa, Oklahoma 74105

918-299-3296 tel
Fax 918-298-7077
1-877-U R GREAT
dawnlawray@aol.com

For over 20 years Randy Carter has been educating, entertaining and inspiring audiences to be their very best. He has risen like the phoenix from the ashes of business failure to fly the friendly skies of success. Your people will grow in both spirit and actions as Randy shares invaluable insights, techniques and principles that are proven to work.

His energetic and entertaining programs, including "Sowing the Seeds of Success," have helped audiences in the millions develop the self-esteem, confidence and direction demanded by today's ever-changing business climate.

Sowing the Seeds of Success

Join Randy as he shares not only the secrets for sowing the right seeds, but also how to cultivate and harvest the "success crop" without getting the fertilizer under your fingernails.

Randy Carter
Delta Communications
1100 80th Ave. SE
Norman, OK 73071

405-321-8859
Fax 405 321-7364
888-239-3768 pin 2976
ralcart@aol.com

Victor T. Costa – "The Natural"

Audiences literally discovered Vic Costa's public speaking gift! Over thirty-two years ago, at the start of his career at Southwestern Bell Telephone he experienced metamorphosis — failure to success! In this process he learned proven success principles that amazed him. As a result, he organized and motivated many below-standard units into top-producing teams.

He works with people to bring out their inherent talent so that they stay excited about reaching their full potential — professionally and personally — even in tough times.

The managers at Bell noticed such phenomenal results and that his enthusiasm was highly contagious. They began to invite him to their meetings as a speaker. Audiences, outside Bell, across the country followed. His inspired message brings positive change to the lives of individuals and organizations. He has been referred to as *"The Will Rogers of the Communications Industry"* and as *"Mr. Verve!"*

Victor T. Costa
Stillwater, Oklahoma
405-624-6002
vtcosta@cowboy.net

ATTITUDE, ATTITUDE, ATTITUDE.

Vern is a veteran motivational speaker who uses humor and unbelievable card tricks that relate to his message. His message is the awesome power of ATTITUDE in safety, sales and personal life. His programs are very entertaining but more importantly, they are effective. He is a member of the National Speakers Association and past president of the Oklahoma Chapter. He is also listed in the *Who's Who In Professional Speaking.*

His clients include many Fortune 500 companies. AMOCO has asked him back 47 times! Audience involvement helps make his programs a roaring success. His motto is: WE'RE HAVING FUN ... BUT WE'RE NOT PLAYING! Vern will defrost your frozen assets! His most requested speeches are: *Attitude is everything; The Keystone of Success (or Safety); and The Magic of__________, (you fill in the blank), There is a Higher Level of Selling.*

Holder & Associates
2005 Running Branch Road
Edmond, Oklahoma 73103

405- 341-1439
1-888-342-2638
SPKRHOLDER@AOL.COM

John Irvin, CSP

John Irvin resides in Tulsa, Oklahoma *(where everything is OK)* and is the president of Lifestyle Enhancement Services (LES), a successful motivational and consulting business.

LES offers keynotes, seminars and workshops that are designed to enhance conferences, conventions, annual meetings, trainings and special events. In fact, LES will make any meeting a special event!

John, a graduate of the University of Tulsa, has been creating "playful opportunities" for personal and professional growth for over twenty-five years. Today, as the creator of *Hilarity Therapy® Programs*, and other programs of "attitude enrichment," John shares from his work in corporate training, leisure sciences, mental health and health and wellness education the message that each of us has the ability to do more and be more than we currently are, and have great fun while doing it!

John Irvin is a member of the American Association for Therapeutic Humor, the National Speakers Association, the Oklahoma Speakers Association, the American Society for Training and Development, the Humor and Health Institute, the Association for Experiential Education, Project Adventure, Inc. and the International Jugglers Association.

John has also authored two joke books, *Chicken Poop In My Bowl* and *Chicken Poop In Your Bowl, II.*

Lifestyle Enhancement Services
P.O. Box 4397
Tulsa, Oklahoma 74159-0397

888-997-PHUN (7486)
jmi1953@ionet.net

Michael Johnson, Ph.D.

Dr. Michael Johnson, author and southern humorist, is a former professional rodeo cowboy who grew up to be an industrial psychologist and university professor. He is the author of a number of books including *The Most Special Person, Susie, The Whispering Horse, Tad Pole and Dr. Frog and Cowboys and Angels*. Stories performed on National Public Radio and Television are offered in a collection of audiotapes: *The Most Special Person, Stories From The South, Stories For Teachers, Stories For Students and Stories For Cowboys.*

Michael is a member of the Board of Directors for the Oklahoma Speakers Association and has performed from Disney World to Canada. Presentations focus on *How To Elicit High Productivity, Rodeo Days* and *F's to A's, Key Behaviors of Unforgettable Leaders* and *The Power Of The Teacher.*

Michael Johnson Productions
159 Oak Hollow
Winthrop, Ar 71866
Toll-Free-877-409-MIKE
Fax-870-381-7289
michaelspeaks@msn.com

Brown Books
16200 N. Dallas Parkway
Suite 225
Dallas, Texas 75248
972-381-0009
publishing@brownbooks.com

Rhett Laubach

Rhett Laubach is president of Kennedy, Laubach & Associates. His company consists of five speakers servicing the youth leadership market through keynotes, workshops and conferences. Rhett credits the Future Farmers of America as his start in a speaking business that afforded him the opportunity to present over 200 keynotes in 1999. He was raised on a farm in Laverne, Oklahoma, and received his Bachelor's degree in Agricultural Economics from Oklahoma State University in May of 1996.

Rhett Laubach
3705 W. 15th
Stillwater, OK 74074

405-372-0094
yournextspeaker@aol.com

Jeff Magee, **Ph.D. / CMC / PDM / CSP**

"He is very good. His message was intellectual, emotional, motivating and timely. Jeff's enthusiasm is contagious; I would not hesitate to recommend him...," Mr. John Coburn, Executive Vice President, The Equitable/AXA Advisors.

Jeff has presented on four continents and in all 50 U.S. states. Ringing endorsements from SAE leaders, Fortune 100 executives, Corporate Universities, to leading government agencies. Everyone agrees that his *managerial-leadership ideas, technologies and approach* "blows-away" audiences and brings about both *immediate results and lasting positive impact*.

A Certified Management Consultant (CMC), this entrepreneur is a six-time best-selling author, international speaker and 1999/2000 President of the Oklahoma Speakers Association who was recently selected as their "Member of the Year 1999!" His programs *"Y2K: Managerial-Leadership Effectiveness©,"* Coaching for Impact©: Generational Leadership", and his powerful *"Conflict Resolution Made Easy©"* are favorites with all audiences!

For more information on scheduling "cutting-edge" technologies on these topics and more as a powerful keynote, results oriented content workshops or one-on-one coaching, call toll free 1-877-90-MAGEE.

Dr. Jeff Magee
P.O. Box 701918
Tulsa, OK 74170-1918

918-495-3626
www.jeffreymagee.com

Carl Potter

Carl Potter is President of Potter and Associates, Inc., a training resource company. Carl works with business people who want to gain more clients. He has been successful in corporate and business life and wishes to pass on the keys to success he has learned through those experiences. If you are looking for high energy, rich content made up of real-life experiences, Carl is your speaker. Participants leave Carl's presentations looking at their business with greater expectations. He is also author of *Thriving Business,* a step-by-step plan for gaining more clients.

Carl Potter
Potter and Associates, Inc.
5815 E. 101st Pl.
Tulsa, OK 74137

918-296-5240
Fax 918-296-5253
Toll Free: 800-259-6209

cpotter924@aol.com
www.potterandassociates.com

Jack R. Pryor

Jack Pryor has been an educator, trainer, and workshop leader for over twenty years and is president of the Pryor Group, Inc. He has a Master's Degree in Industrial Education from Oklahoma State University and his postgraduate work is in management.

Jack has worked with business and industries helping them to develop strategic directions and find strategic solutions to their unique problems. Jack helped design the strategic planning model for the Oklahoma Technology Centers and has used this model successfully with other nonprofit organizations. When Jack facilitates a strategic plan for an organization he believes in developing a clear and vivid vision of where the organization wants to be.

He has made numerous presentations at state, regional and national conferences. He has delivered workshops for nonprofit organizations and business and industries as diverse as the Yukon Chamber of Commerce, Fiserv, City Bites Inc., Xerox, Delta Faucet Co., Resurrection Lutheran Church, Oklahoma Department of Vocational-Technical Education, Spanish Cove Retirement Village, King's Gamebirds Inc., Oklahoma Alliance for Manufacturing Excellence, Oklahoma Community Institute and the Oklahoma Workforce Development system.

Jack Pryor
The Pryor Group
P.O. Box 851435
Yukon, OK 73085-1435

405-354-1604
pryorgp@ icnet.net

Mary J. Pryor

Mary J. Pryor is an award-winning writer, speaker, and video producer. She is a skilled communicator who gets her point across with humor and a human touch. Audiences of all sizes find Mary's messages creative and packed with energy.

Mary's first book, *Start Now! Life Is Too Short*, is now in its second printing. Its companion piece, *More Inspiration on the Subject!* was published in 1999. Mary is also the author of *Jelly Side Up! Finding Time for What's Important in Your Life*.

She's a member of the National Speakers Association and a founding member of the Pryor Group — a company dedicated to building people personally and professionally through training in motivation, communication, planning, and goal setting. Let Mary inspire and motivate you!

The Pryor Group
Mary J. Pryor
P.O. Box 851435
Yukon, Oklahoma 73085-1435

(405) 354-1604
pryorgp@icnet.net

Kent A. Rader

Kent Rader works with organizations who want to increase profits by developing happier, healthier employees. Kent's programs on life balance, stress reduction and team building are derived from his management experience as C.E.O. and C.F.O. of healthcare organizations. This experience is uniquely compiled with that of a life-long competitive runner and humor to offer participants a wealth of information in an entertaining environment. His passion is sharing with empowering organizations the knowledge that healthy and happy employees lead to success and profits via employee retention and more-creative problem solving skills! He has presented his programs to groups throughout the United States who want to make a positive difference in the lives of their employees.

Kent Rader
Competitive Advantage
715 North Oklahoma
Mangum, Oklahoma 73554

405-209-3273
CompetitiveAdvan@aol.com

R. Michael "Mike" Ruckel

Mike is a highly successful, award-winning salesman and inspiring professional speaker. He has earned many sales awards and speaks before sales organizations, business and professional groups, and some not-so-professional groups. Mike has even gone to prison to conduct education programs for the inmates.

Mike is a Charter Member and Past President of the Oklahoma Speakers Association and has been an active member of the National Speakers Association since 1984. Mike has been published in *The Toastmaster* magazine and has achieved Toastmasters' highest speaking and leadership designation.

Mike Ruckel
Ruckel Communications
P.O. Box 12607
Oklahoma City, OK 73157-2607

405-722-7494

After retiring from the F.B.I., Mike organized and supervised a health care fraud investigative unit for the Oklahoma Attorney General. Looking for something different, Wow!, did he find it! At age 54, Mike became an award-winning Flight Attendant with American Airlines. After seven years with American, Mike chose to retire and keep those notorious airline passes! With three college degrees (business, religious studies, and a master's in criminal justice) and varied and unique experiences, Mike began speaking professionally. Combining humor, motivation and information, Mike speaks on *"Providing Dynamic Customer Service!" "Preventing Workplace Violence!" "Making Lives A Success!"* and *"Successful Marriages, Successful Families!"* Mike uses entertaining experiences from high school, college, the U.S. Marine Corps, the F.B.I., the airline and his family to make important points in his interactive presentations.

Impact Presentations
2604 Echo Trail
Edmond, OK 73013-6732

405.341.8414
Fax 405.341.8560

exfed@worldnet.aft.net
www.MikeSeikel.com

Jim Stovall

Jim Stovall has been a national champion Olympic weightlifter, a successful investment broker, and entrepreneur. He is Co-Founder and President of the Narrative Television Network, which makes movies and television accessible for our nation's 13 million blind and visually impaired people and their families. Although originally designed for the blind and visually impaired, over 60 percent of NTN's nationwide audience is made up of fully sighted people who simply enjoy the programming.

Jim Stovall hosts the Network's talk show, *NTN Showcase*. His guests have included Katharine Hepburn, Jack Lemmon, Carol Channing, Steve Allen, and Eddie Albert, as well as many others. The Narrative Television Network has received an Emmy Award and an International Film and Video Award among its many industry honors.

NTN has grown to include over 1,200 cable systems and broadcast stations, reaching over 35 million homes in the United States, and NTN is shown in 11 foreign countries. NTN programming is also presented via the Internet at NarrativeTV.com, serving millions of people around the world.

Jim Stovall joined the ranks of Walt Disney, Orson Welles, and four United States presidents when he was selected as one of the "Ten Outstanding Young Americans" by the U.S. Junior Chamber of Commerce. He has appeared on *Good Morning America* and CNN, and has been featured in *Reader's Digest*, *TV Guide*, and *Time* magazine. He is the author of previous books entitled *You Don't Have To Be Blind To See*, *Success Secrets of Super Achievers*, and *The Way I See The World*, as well as his new book *The Ultimate Gift*. The President's Committee on Equal Opportunity selected Jim Stovall as the 1997 Entrepreneur of the Year.

Jim Stovall
5840 S. Memorial Drive
Suite 312
Tulsa, OK 74145-9082

918-627-1000
Fax: 918-627-4101
JimStovall@aol.com